The Spirituality of
Mark

The Spirituality of
Mark

RESPONDING TO GOD

Mitzi Minor

Westminster John Knox Press
Louisville, Kentucky

Scripture quotations from the New Revised Standard Version of the Bible are copyright © 1989 by the Division of Christian Education of the National Council of the Churches of Christ in the U.S.A. and are used by permission. Most scripture quotations are the author's own translations from the Greek.

Book design by Jennifer K. Cox
Cover design by Alec Bartsch
Cover illustration: Lion in Majesty *by Michele Giambono. Correr Civic Museum, Venice, M. Magliani. Courtesy SuperStock.*

First edition

Published by Westminster John Knox Press
Louisville, Kentucky

This book is printed on acid-free paper that meets the American National Standards Institute Z39.48 standard. ∞

PRINTED IN THE UNITED STATES OF AMERICA

96 97 98 99 00 01 02 03 04 05 — 10 9 8 7 6 5 4 3 2 1

Library of Congress Cataloging-in-Publication Data

Minor, Mitzi, date.
    The spirituality of Mark : responding to God / Mitzi Minor — 1st ed.
        p.   cm.
    Includes bibliographical references and index.
    ISBN 0-664-25679-1 (alk. paper)
    1. Bible. N.T. Mark—Criticism, interpretation, etc.
2. Spiritual life—Biblical teaching.   3. Christian life—Biblical
teaching.   I. Title
BS2585.6.S65M56   1996
226.3′06—dc20   96-17778

For Georgia Minor and Larry Minor,
who first taught me to respond to God

Contents

Preface

Having grown up in a genuine, churchgoing family, having been part of an active youth group in my church, I have wonderful memories of the ways the Bible intersected my life. I remember a fascination in second grade with the stories of Abraham, Isaac, Jacob, and Joseph (especially that many-colored coat). I remember "discovering" Matthew 11:28 ("Come to me, all of you who are weary and heavy laden . . .") during some tough teenage times. I once read the Acts of the Apostles through in one sitting, as captivated by its story as by any adventure novel. In college, during some days when I was seeing, for the first time through more adult eyes, how harsh the world can be, I clung to Colossians 1:17 ("He is before all things and in him all things hold together").

Consequently, I was not surprised, nor were the people who knew me well, when during my seminary years my sense of vocation moved steadily in the direction of studying for a Ph.D. in New Testament. I was surprised, however, when my study was under way to discover that so much of academic biblical scholarship was not interested in the types of questions about truth and faith and life that had always made me interested in the New Testament. Often I finished a scholarly book or article and found myself asking, So what? No wonder the church and the academy have had too little to do with one another (I thought).

Fortunately, from my perspective, I discovered some scholars who had similar concerns—scholars like Sandra Schneiders and Walter Wink. Fortunately, I was studying with professors—Gerald Borchert, Alan Culpepper, Jim Blevins, and Glenn Hinson—who allowed me to voice my concerns and pursue my interests, however tentatively, in a dissertation titled "The Spirituality of the Gospel of Mark." Fortunately, I've found since completion of my degree in 1989 that liberationist biblical scholars have similar criticisms of traditional academic biblical scholarship.

This book, therefore, is the fruit of those original interests, the benefits from and the frustrations with the academy, the insights gained from scholars who have questions similar to mine, and my own "living with" Mark's Gospel since the fall of 1986. I would now describe my dissertation as the embryonic form of this book, which I hope is a more mature perspective on Mark's spirituality.

Readers should know two other things about this work. The first is simple: Most biblical quotations are my own translations of the Greek.

Second, this nearly ten-year journey could only have happened with the aid of some wonderful people. Among my Southern Baptist Theological Seminary connections, Gerald Borchert supervised the dissertation and so had the first role in helping my thoughts come to life. Alan Culpepper's help on the dissertation meant that it was better organized and more clearly thought out. David May first got me interested in Mark's Gospel and the possibilities there, and he has continued to share ideas and offer critical comments on work I have done. Chris Church has listened to me think out loud, watched me pull my hair out (figuratively speaking, of course), heard me moan when a section would not come together, read many pages and offered critical comments, and even endured me when I got defensive about his critical comments. He has done everything a "best friend" ought to do.

Among my Memphis Theological Seminary connections, I am particularly grateful to my dean, Don McKim, for all his support and encouragement. Every faculty should have a dean like Don. Special thanks go to Mary Lin Hudson for the years of friendship and encouragement. My other MTS colleagues have been supportive as well, reading portions of the manuscript, listening to my ideas, and offering feedback. The help and support of the library staff has been invaluable, as has the enthusiasm with which my students have responded to my perspective on Mark. To all my MTS family I say thank you.

My editor at Westminster John Knox Press, Jon Berquist, has certainly gone the second mile in seeing this project to completion. To Jon I owe a tremendous debt of gratitude.

Finally, I wish to thank my family, but I have no idea how. My parents read Bible stories to me as a child, encouraged my burgeoning faith as a teenager, supported me through graduate school, and share my excitement about this project's publication. How does anyone say thanks for all that? The best that I can do is dedicate this book to them. My sisters and I shared our growing pains and growing faith and managed to make sure we came out sane. Today they share their kids with me—Ashley, Tyler, Courtney, Ryan, and Carter—so that I am reminded constantly of the importance of nurturing an authentic Christian spirituality that can make God's world a better place for them. That's what this book is about.

Mark's Gospel
and the
Life of Faith

The New Testament is a collection of faith documents, that is, documents written "from faith to faith" in order to transform ordinary human beings into persons living new lives of great faith in God's purposes in Jesus the Christ.[1] Until readers are so transformed by the New Testament, they have not encountered it as its writers intended.

Many, perhaps most, Christians need neither biblical scholars nor theologians to explain to them that this is the purpose of the New Testament. Instead many Christians instinctively turn to the Bible again and again to nurture their faith, to deepen their understanding of God and their experience of God in order to be transformed and have their Christian commitment renewed.

In my college years and just afterward, my favorite part of the New Testament was the Gospel of John. Many seminary students in my introductory New Testament classes today also name John as their favorite New Testament book. The long discourses Jesus offers in John about light and darkness, good and evil, life and death, truth, the assurance of God's abiding presence, and the primacy of love for Christians offer helpful answers to people of faith who are trying to make sense out of life.

Other Christians, however, are enamored of Paul. His calls to live by the Spirit and walk by faith (not by sight), his wrestling within himself because "I do not do the good I want, but the evil I do not want is what I do," his ringing assertion that "the wages of sin is death, but the free gift of God is eternal life in Christ," and his image of the church as the body of Christ inspire these Christians to fight the good fight of faithful lives.

Still other Christians find themselves most challenged by Matthew's

1

version of Jesus' Sermon on the Mount, or most interested in the
teachings on prayer in Luke, or most intrigued by the apocalyptic visions of the Revelation to John. Other than those who have completed
seminary classes, I have yet to meet someone whose favorite New Testament book is Mark.[2]

By contrast, New Testament scholars have long been greatly interested in the Second Gospel. Most of them believe Mark was the first
Gospel written and was later used as a source by Matthew and Luke.
If this hypothesis is true, then Mark was the creator of the gospel genre.
Scholars wonder about the implications of Mark's choosing to tell a
story of Jesus instead of writing a theological treatise about Jesus. Questions regarding the identity of this author,[3] his literary style, Christology, theology of suffering, the role of the disciples in his story, the
strange ending to the Gospel, and the like have kept the minds of
scholars stewing for most of this century.

All this scholarly attention on Mark, however, does not appear to
have stimulated great interest in Mark among Christian nonscholars,
who are usually more concerned about transformed lives and nurture
for their faith. Does this mean that Mark has little to teach Christians
about how to live their lives of faith? I wish to answer that question
with an emphatic no! In fact, I believe Mark offers a profound perspective on what it means to be Christian.

What has happened with regard to Mark, in my estimation, is that
Christian nonscholars do not find in the Second Gospel long teaching
sections "laying out" how they should live (like those they find in the
Sermon on the Mount or John or Paul), and scholars have not taught
them how to discern the implications of choosing to follow Christ
from a narrative text like Mark.[4] The result has been a great underappreciation of all that Mark has to offer Christians seeking to nurture
their faith.

With this book I hope to begin to correct this underappreciation
of the Second Gospel's gifts to the life of faith. Accordingly, this study
is about the experience of God captured in Mark's Gospel and how
Mark believed Christians should respond to such an experience.

Many scholars would call this effort an exercise in biblical spirituality, a relatively new but growing area of study that is interested in the
things I have just mentioned: the experiences of God that are recorded
in the biblical texts and the responses these experiences provoked in
the people who had them. The belief that such experiences and responses are key components of the biblical texts derives from a theo-

logical understanding of the Bible as revelation of God. The insights of several scholars enable us to appreciate the significance of these ideas. Sandra Schneiders has noted this:

> Scripture, according to Christian tradition, is a record of revelation. Revelation is the encounter between the self-giving God and the actively receptive human being. In other words, divine revelation is, by nature, a spiritual experience if considered from the human point of view.[5]

With regard to the New Testament, Sharyn Dowd claimed that those whose witness is preserved in its pages understood their theological statements to be "reflections on and expressions of their spirituality— of their encounters with and experience of the God who was made known in Jesus Christ."[6] Carolyn Osiek maintained that the New Testament bears witness to the variety of ways in which people have heard God's call to live a life of faith and fidelity.[7] Stephen Barton declared the Gospels to be "classic expressions of Christian spirituality," and that "they are shaped through and through by a sense of the presence of God in Christ, and they are deeply serious attempts to re-envisage the whole of life in response."[8] Louis Bouyer described the four Gospels similarly:

> Far from being rudimentary biographies interspersed with collections of Jesus' sayings, these Gospels already testify, by their choice and presentation of words and deeds, to a process of ordered reflection. In particular . . . they express formed spiritualities. The image of Jesus which they communicate to us reflects, with each one of them, a particular spiritual experience.[9]

Clearly, the New Testament teaching about God has its roots in these early Christians' experiences of God and their responses to these experiences, or, we might say, in these early Christians' spirituality.

Christians today who continue to turn to the New Testament for spiritual nurture often hope to foster (though they may not use these words) an authentic New Testament spirituality in the present. A first consideration in achieving this goal is that they not abuse the New Testament in their endeavors. Too many Christians have been guilty of such abuse in the past. They have used the New Testament to justify slave ownership, to insist that wives be submissive and remain married to abusive husbands, to promote a private, spiritualized piety that has little impact on the world around them. If Christians would use (and not abuse) the New Testament today, they must be part of Christian communities whose responses to God are founded on those of the Christian communities that originally produced the New Testament texts.[10] This, then, underscores the importance of carefully and critically studying the spirituality of the New Testament texts today.

A second consideration in achieving the goal of fostering an authentic New Testament spirituality in the present is that the whole spectrum of the experiences of God reflected in the New Testament be appreciated and evaluated in order to be appropriated by the church. Too much focus on the Johannine and Pauline writings produces an unbalanced view of New Testament spirituality. Christians also need to know about Luke-Acts, the Catholic epistles, and similar texts. I must be content here to contribute to correcting any such imbalance by uncovering Mark's experience of God for Christians to understand and consider.

To accomplish this, I need to clarify the precise goals of this study and how it will be organized to meet these goals. I have been speaking about experiences of God and responses to these, but I need to explain how these ideas and the notion of spirituality fit together in a study of a narrative text like Mark. This task is crucial because of the ambiguity that often surrounds ideas about spirituality. Broader than a theology or a set of values, spirituality has been called a glob area because it is often considered to be all-encompassing and pervasive, reaching into one's depths and touching those surest human feelings and convictions about the way things really are. When viewed this way, spirituality could be everywhere, and yet, because of that pervasiveness, it can seem to be nowhere. Since its scope is potentially as vast as the sum and depth of all human experience, workable content for critical study of spirituality can virtually disappear. Indeed, spirituality is famous for a noticeable lack of tools for organizing its vast resources. The result, too often, is vagueness when defining itself.[11]

In order to make workable content reappear, spirituality scholar Edward Kinerk proposed three distinctions that should be included in a focused working definition of spirituality. The definition should (1) limit the material to what is expressed; (2) include the idea of personal growth; and (3) contain what he called "markers"—his are "expressions of the authentic and inauthentic." Thus his working definition is, "A spirituality . . . is the expression of a dialectical personal growth from the inauthentic to the authentic."[12] I wish to examine each of these three distinctions for the help they offer a study of Mark.

Kinerk's insistence on limiting the material to what is expressed may appear to be a statement of the obvious, but the distinction is important. Spirituality is concerned with the spiritual experience of God, but experiences can only be studied indirectly by analyzing the expressions (i.e., the written records) of the experiences. Interestingly, Kinerk does not include "experience of God" in his definition. I will follow the lead of many scholars who include this idea in the definition to be used to study Mark.[13] Furthermore, noting that the experience of God is through Christ makes the spirituality being defined a specifically Christian spirituality.

Kinerk's inclusion of personal growth is a welcome addition to many definitions of spirituality. Certainly we expect that spiritual masters write to encourage their readers to grow in their relationships to God. Also, Kinerk described this growth as dialectical because all spiritual growth is a simultaneous yes to one thing and a no to something else: "Each step toward the authentic demands a corresponding rejection of the inauthentic."[14] This idea of dialectical personal growth is maintained in my working definition to be used with Mark.

Kinerk's third distinction calls for the definition to have "markers." Thus he claimed that personal spiritual growth occurs when a person moves from the inauthentic toward the authentic. But authentic what? Inauthentic what? I find help in clarifying Kinerk's idea from the German scholar Adolf Deissmann, who claimed that Christian spirituality is a reacting spirituality, a *response* to God's initiatives.[15] Similarly, Denise Lardner Carmody has observed that the initiative of the love of God, rather than the anxious questioning of the human seeker, was what captivated the interest of the prophets in the scriptures.[16] Therefore, "authentic responses to God's initiatives" and "inauthentic responses to God's initiatives" are clearer markers than merely "authentic" and "inauthentic," and they are added to the definition used here.

In order to be as precise as possible, I must now ask, What constitutes a response to God? The following list is composed from the work of various scholars of things that should be considered responses to God: images of God, images of self and others, images of the world, and perspectives about history, attitudes, values, beliefs, emotions, and activities.[17]

Kinerk's two adjectives, authentic and inauthentic, are maintained. Since "authentic" can indicate that something derives from a trusted source, these adjectives in this study will designate those responses that are judged by Mark as truly of God (authentic) and those that are judged as not of God (inauthentic).

good of bk

Thus we arrive at the working definition of Christian spirituality to
be applied to Mark's narrative: It is the expression of the experience
of God through Jesus Christ, which calls believers to dialectical personal growth moving from inauthentic responses to God's initiatives
toward authentic responses to God's initiatives.

Using this working definition of spirituality, we will search through
what Mark has written for the experience of God in Christ Jesus reflected there and for the responses to God that Mark judged as authentic or inauthentic. In so doing, we will be able to understand the
spirituality of the Second Gospel and how it may nurture and challenge Christians today as they seek to live their faith in Christ.

Chapter 1

Searching for Mark's Spirituality

Now that we know what we are seeking in Mark's Gospel, we must determine how to find it. Again the task is more difficult than might first be imagined. When studying the writings of spiritual masters such as Catherine of Siena or John of the Cross, we have access to their specific exhortations to their disciples to grow in faith and, frequently, to personal reminiscences of their own spiritual experiences from which to understand their spiritualities. The Gospels, however, present a different challenge. On the one hand, we do not learn directly from the Gospels about the religious experiences of the writers or the communities from which the Gospels came or to which they were directed. Instead, we must analyze the ways in which a Gospel writer told the story of Jesus and infer from that story the basic outlook which that writer had about God and how that outlook reflects his or her own spiritual experiences.[1] On the other hand, good stories are true to human experience and depend for their power on successfully illuminating significant areas of human experience.[2] Because narrative and experience are so closely related, stories such as Mark's should present fine opportunities for understanding and sharing in others' experiences. So, we need a method of study that will allow us to infer from Mark's story of Jesus what Mark's own spirituality was. In addition, we need to organize and analyze that spirituality. The purpose of this chapter is to present a method of study that will enable us to accomplish these goals.

Tools for Analyzing Mark's Spirituality

The primary means of discovering Mark's spirituality will be to answer a rather obvious question drawn from our definition of spirituality:

What are the initiatives of God and the authentic and inauthentic responses they generate in Mark's story? But what tools will enable us to
answer this question? First, we need some initial questions to ask about
the text that will show us God's initiatives and the responses to these.
We can return to the work of Edward Kinerk for help in formulating
these questions. Plus, the Second Gospel itself suggests some additions
to Kinerk's work that make for a clearer understanding of God's initiatives and the responses these provoke. Second, the tools of redaction, narrative, and sociological criticisms will enable us to appreciate
the world of the text and, thus, answer our questions. Finally, after we
have understood the world of the text, we need to ask some additional
questions that will help us draw conclusions and understand the spirituality that Mark's story invites readers to share.[3] When all these tasks
and perspectives are combined, we find that we need to understand
the following: (1) the role of the Markan Jesus, (2) questions to ask
about the text, (3) an organizing form for Mark's spirituality, and (4)
questions to help us draw conclusions.

The Role of the Markan Jesus

As the author of a narrative text, Mark communicates with readers
through the text's narrator. Scholars using the tools of narrative criti-
cism have noted that through his narrator Mark has colored his story
with an evaluative point of view. That is, he slants the story in favor
of certain attitudes, beliefs, values, and norms that he shares with the
central character, Jesus. Furthermore, Mark not only identified his
own evaluative point of view with that of Jesus, he also made certain
that his and Jesus' evaluative points of view are presented as being in
accord with God.[4] Therefore, Mark presents Jesus' way of responding
to God and Jesus' evaluations of others' responses to God as the key to
judging which responses in the story are authentic and which are not.
By paying attention to this critical role of Jesus, we will learn much
about Mark's spirituality.

Questions to Ask about the Text

To uncover the authentic and inauthentic responses to God's initiatives in Mark, we should ask the following questions of Mark's story.
First, what are the initiatives God takes in Mark? These initiatives may
be discovered by noting what Jesus says God has done, what Mark narrates God as doing, and/or by noting what action of God is implied

by the way people respond in a given situation. Second, what are the competing responses to these initiatives? When these have been noted, we can then determine which ones Mark displaces by relating that Jesus rebuked, condemned, criticized, or warned against them (remembering the critical role of Jesus). Further, we can discover other responses that Mark displaces by describing them in such a way that they contradict Jesus' responses or the responses of others that Jesus has already approved. After these negative considerations come positive ones. Which of the competing responses does Mark affirm and elevate by noting that Jesus commanded, expected, or praised them? Which ones are elevated by being described so that they correspond to Jesus' responses or to responses that Jesus has already approved? When answers to these questions have been found, then the first summaries of Markan spirituality may be compiled.

An Organizing Form
for Mark's Spirituality

The goal of this study is not merely to list the expressions of authentic and inauthentic responses but also to organize and analyze them. Thus we should put them into some organizing form that gives the responses depth and relationship to one another. Kinerk gives an example of such a form from Ignatius Loyola's *Spiritual Exercises:* the kingdom of Christ versus the kingdom of Satan. He claimed, "The Kingdom of Christ gives depth and relationship to the expressions of the authentic while the Kingdom of Satan does the same for the inauthentic."[5] Mark contains an organizing form that has a similar structure: whenever the conflict at the heart of Mark's story is named *explicitly,* it is named as being between God and humanity. In 7:8 Jesus accused the scribes and Pharisees: "Having left the commandment of God, you hold fast to human tradition."[6] In 8:33, after Jesus' first passion prediction, Jesus rebuked Peter for not accepting suffering for the gospel as God's will, saying, "You are not thinking the things of God but of humanity." In 11:27 the chief priests, scribes, and elders came to Jesus demanding to know by whose authority Jesus had cleansed the Temple. Jesus responded with his own question (11:30): "Was the baptism of John from heaven or of human origin?" Finally, in 12:14, the Pharisees and Herodians came to trap Jesus and addressed him in flattering words dripping with ironic truth: "You do not look on the outward appearance of humans, but in truth you are teaching the way of God." New Testament scholar Norman Petersen claimed that for Mark there were two ways of perceiving things, one right and one wrong, one divine and one human. The divine way is the one taken by Mark and Jesus.[7] Thus the organizing form for Mark's spirituality is *the Way of the Lord versus the Way of Humanity*.

The term "way of the Lord" is taken from Mark 1:2–3: "Behold I am sending my messenger before your face who will prepare your way; a voice crying in the wilderness: Prepare *the way of the Lord,* make straight his paths" (emphasis mine). From this moment in the story "the way" is a significant motif in Mark's Gospel. It occurs in important places at 6:8 when the Twelve go out on their own missionary travels, near all three passion predictions (8:27, 9:34, and 10:32), and at 10:52 when Bartimaeus responds to being healed by following Jesus "on the way" to Jerusalem and the cross. Because of the importance of this motif, it is also used in the name given to inauthentic spirituality in Mark (the Way of Humanity). Interestingly, "way" and "journey" (which is how the Greek word for "way" is sometimes translated) are also important motifs in the writings of many mystics and spiritual masters.

Questions to
Help Us Draw Conclusions

When we have found the authentic and inauthentic responses, then we must analyze them by asking some questions about the initial summaries of the responses. The answers to these questions should enable us to draw conclusions regarding Mark's spirituality. The initial question concerns Mark's experience of God: What descriptions, pictures, or images of God emerge from the initiatives of God that were found? These images are important for learning how Mark felt about God since his language about God is sober and reserved. He most often speaks of God without attributes or ascriptions.[8] We should also ask if any of these images is so bound by first-century ideology, worldview, or culture that we need not, even must not, appropriate them today. The simplest questions regarding the responses are: What responses make up authentic spirituality according to Mark? Which ones make up inauthentic spirituality? We might also want to keep in mind such questions as: Do some responses emerge as being particularly significant? Do the responses from the various sections of Mark mesh with one another? Are there contradictions? Are these responses "appropriate-able" for us today? We may also ask a question prompted by the proposed organizing form for Mark's spirituality: Does it fit Mark's whole Gospel? If so, does Mark indicate why inauthentic spirituality should be dubbed the Way of Humanity? The answers to these questions should offer a clear picture of the spirituality Mark believes in and invites us to share.

Passages Selected for Study

The Gospel of Mark, like many spiritual writings, is too long to be examined all at once. Therefore, we must select representative sections that can be related to the whole Gospel. Kinerk, who again provides aid in making these selections, noted, "To discover the wisdom of a particular spirituality we must look at its teachings."[9] Study of teachings is particularly appropriate, because one of Mark's favorite designations for Jesus is Teacher.

The three main teaching sections in Mark's Gospel are 4:1–34; 7:1–23; and 13:1–37. In addition, an important set of teachings from Mark's discipleship section (8:27–10:52), namely, Jesus' three passion predictions and the responses to these (8:31–9:1; 9:30–37; and 10:32–45), are selected for study. Each of these sections contains themes of Mark's spirituality that appear throughout the Gospel. We will review these other appearances as well.

Mark has emphasized in his story, however, that Jesus taught not only by what he said but also by what he did. In 1:21–28 an exorcism by Jesus is called a "new teaching with power." In 6:2 the wisdom of his teachings is linked with "the mighty works done by his hands." Therefore, we will study a select group of Jesus' miracles along with his discourses to grasp the full measure of Jesus' teachings in Mark. The miracle recorded in 3:1–6 is representative of the healings of Jesus and the climax of the first group of miracle stories in Mark (2:1–3:6). The nature miracle of 4:35–41 is representative of the second miracle group Mark narrates (4:35–5:43). Two of the many exorcisms in Mark are chosen. The first, 7:24–30, occurs during Jesus' first travels beyond Galilee and involves women and distance. The second, 9:14–29, occurs on the journey to Jerusalem (8:27–10:52) where, in contrast to the first half of the Gospel, only two miracles occur. Finally, the cursing of the fig tree in 11:12–25 is chosen because of its uniqueness among the miracles, its relationship to prayer, and its occurrence during passion week. As with the discourse sections, we will observe and review the themes of Mark's spirituality that appear in these passages.

Summary

The method for studying Mark's spirituality proposed in this chapter involves relying on the insights from redaction, narrative, and sociological criticisms to help us understand the world of the text. We will focus on the role of Jesus, an organizing form for Mark's spirituality, questions to ask the text, and questions to help us draw conclusions to enable us to grasp the world Mark wishes us to enter. We will use this method to analyze nine representative passages in Mark (3:1–6; 4:1–34; 4:35–41; 7:1–23; 7:24–30; 8:31–9:1, 9:14–29; 9:30–37, 10:32–45; 11:12–25; 13:1–37). When we have concluded these tasks, we will have a picture of the spirituality Mark advocates and invites us to join.

Chapter 2

Responding to God Who Reveals Mystery and True Purity

Jesus spends much time and energy teaching the people about the way of the Lord in Mark. He teaches in the synagogue, by the sea, in the house, and on the way. Always, according to Mark, he teaches them by means of parables (4:34). To understand Jesus' teachings in Mark, therefore, we must first understand what is meant by *parable* in Mark.

Parable does not denote a fixed form of speech for Mark. On the basis of its Hebrew and Greek origins, it could describe any speech that was out of the ordinary or in some way striking. Mark used the flexibility of the term to designate as parables all the more significant forms of speech, such as wisdom sayings, riddles, brief stories, which Jesus employed in speaking to the multitudes. But Mark pushed the term further: He inferred that not only spoken words but also events could be parabolic. The actions of Jesus were conceived as having a hidden religious significance like the spoken parables, so that through them also the mystery of the kingdom of God found expression.[1] For the purposes of this chapter the significant implication of linking Jesus' actions with his words is that his words are also to be equated with his miraculous acts because they are that powerful.

> Jesus' teaching, then, is for the Second Evangelist an act of divine power; while Matthew and Luke clearly distinguished between miracles and teachings, Mark sees both activities as one and the same manifestation of this power. We could say that the word which teaches is the same word which expels the demon.[2]

Furthermore, the parables that Jesus spoke were more than pedagogical aids for would-be disciples. Due to the mysteriousness of parables, there was no more appropriate way for him to speak of the mystery of

13

the kingdom of God. New Testament scholar John R. Donahue made an observation about parables that is especially significant for a study of Mark's spirituality. Drawing on C. H. Dodd's classic definition of parable (a metaphor or simile drawn from nature or common life that arrests the hearer by its vividness or strangeness and leaves the mind in sufficient doubt about its precise application to tease it into active thought[3]), Donahue held that the metaphoric quality of a parable is especially suited to express two qualities of religious experience: immediacy and transcendence.

> A religious experience—that sense of awe in the face of the holy or of being grasped by mystery—is always immediate and individual, and in the great religious literature of human history it is expressed in physical and sensuous imagery.[4]

The physical and sensuous imagery of Jesus' parables—those metaphors or similes drawn from nature or common life—serve to bring the mystery of God closer to us. It does so by juxtaposing what were thought to be incomparable elements like the kingdom of God and a mustard seed, so that one's imagination is tricked into seeing a new vision of reality. The secret strategy of the parables is to seduce by means of the ordinary with a view toward the extraordinary. Through their world-subverting discourse, parables invite hearers into what appears to be a simple story and through it to the truer story behind the story.[5] The result is that Jesus' parables summon his hearers to see ordinary, everyday life in a new way as the carrier of the presence of God.

Here is a good place to be reminded of the worldview of the first Christians. The ancients believed that there is, in addition to the visible, material world, another level of reality, a second world of nonmaterial reality, a "spiritual world" charged with energy and power. Furthermore, they believed that this other world could be experienced since the spirit world and the world of ordinary experience could intersect at a number of points.[6] In his parables, Jesus proclaimed that God had intersected the world of God's people again, but this time in a new way: This time God's kingdom had drawn near. People who were anticipating "the way things had always been" only better would be surprised. Jesus' words were powerful not because of aesthetic brilliance or paradoxical quality but because of the unexpected experience of God mediated by them.[7] In this chapter we are seeking this experience of God in Mark 4:1–34 and 7:1–23.

Mark 4:1–34

Jesus' first public act in Mark was to enter the synagogue at Caper-
naum and teach (1:21–28). The people there were astonished at both
his words and his exorcism of a demon. They called the whole experience a "new teaching with authority" (1:27). What Jesus taught is
not revealed in this story, however. The first full-length presentation
of Jesus' teaching does not come until the parable discourse of 4:1–34.
After a series of rapidly moving, loosely connected events leading to
this point (note, e.g., the rapidity of the five episodes in 2:1–3:6), Mark
suddenly fixes the time and place of his story for a while in a boat on
the sea (4:1) and pauses as if to say, "Look, we have to stop and pay
attention now!"[8]

Mark appears to be responsible for bringing together various sayings of Jesus to form the single long discourse of 4:1–34.[9] The result
of his editorial work is a carefully composed discourse presented in
concentric (or circular) parallels that may be outlined as follows:

A		4:1–2	Introduction
	B	4:3–9	Sower Parable
	C	4:10–13	Reason for Parables Given to Disciples
	D	4:14–20	Interpretation of a Parable Given to Disciples
	C′	4:21–25	Mysterious Sayings Given to Disciples
	B′	4:26–32	Seed Parables
A′		4:33–34	Conclusion[10]

The initial striking element of Mark's composition is that the introduction, conclusion, and parables frame the material that is most
clearly addressed to disciples (C D C′). As the center of the discourse,
these words to disciples (vv. 10–25) occupy a "hinge" position in the
structure and, thus, an emphasized place in this teaching by Mark's
Jesus. We begin our study with this emphatic material addressed to
disciples.

Verses 10–13:
God's Initiative

After the public teaching of the sower parable, "those who were
around him along with the twelve" (Mark implies elsewhere also that
the group of disciples was always larger than the Twelve; note, e.g.,

10:52, 15:40–41) ask Jesus in private about the parables (4:10), referring not only to the parable he had just told (4:3–9) but to any and
perhaps all of his teachings to this point. Jesus tells them about the parables and, in the process, about God: "To you the mystery of the kingdom of God has been given; but to those outside all things are in parables" (v. 11). *Mystery* refers to something known only by God and that
God alone can reveal. The Jewish background of the word indicates
something that can be well known but only to those to whom God
chooses to give knowledge while in the New Testament "mystery"
means "an 'open secret' made known by God."[11] Significantly, Jesus
does not explain God's kingdom in these verses. Instead he tells disciples that God is revealing it to them. Thus we understand that God has
taken the initiative to reveal through Jesus what has heretofore been
mysterious and unknown about God's kingdom to disciples.

The content of the mystery is the *basileia* of God, a Greek word that
is difficult to translate because it can mean kingdom (the usual choice
in translations of the New Testament and, thus, the one with which
we are most familiar), kingly realm, domain, empire, monarchy, kingly
rule, sovereignty, dominion, or reign. First-century Mediterranean
people were likely to think of the Roman Empire when they heard
the word. Imagine the effect, therefore, of attributing the *basileia* to
God![12] The mystery, as it will unfold in Mark's story, is that God's
basileia has drawn near as Jesus had proclaimed (1:15) and has become
operative in Jesus' mission.[13] In other words, God has taken the initiative—here is another one—to launch God's *basileia* through the
words, works, and destiny of Jesus. Thus there is an alternative to living under Roman rule: One can live within the domain of God's exercise of power that is experientially available now. This domain is still
a mystery because it is currently hidden. Indeed it does not appear to
be present at all, but Mark's Jesus insists it is. It is only waiting to manifest itself in power (see 9:1).

How then should we translate *basileia?* Choosing one of the above
options eliminates the others and loses the possibilities and ambiguity
of the word. Furthermore, most of the above options ascribe imperial
power to God which, as we will see, is exactly how God does not exercise power according to Mark. Following the lead of Elisabeth
Schüssler Fiorenza, therefore, I choose from here on simply to translit-
erate the word as *basileia,* thus allowing it to evoke its whole range of
meanings.[14]

A final aspect of God's initiative in these verses is that God reveals the mystery only to disciples or insiders. To those outside "all things are in parables" (v. 11). The use of "parables" in this verse emphasizes that the sayings are shrouded in darkness to those not close to Jesus, who will not do the will of God, whose hearts are already hardened, who will not see or hear.[15] For such people the parables are for the purpose of preventing repentance (v. 12). Isaiah 6:9 is used here, a text in which the power of the prophetic word is depicted as reaching the hearts of Israelites and hardening them against submitting to the word of God. Mark's Jesus understood the prophetic word in substantially the same way.[16] Thus the result of Jesus' parables is that some people see Jesus but do not really see him. They hear his words but do not understand them (v. 12). These people remain outsiders. God's initiative, therefore, also involves distinguishing true disciples by giving God's word about the mysterious *basileia* of God. The parabolic quality of God's word does not so much cause persons to be outsiders as expose both those whose hearts are hardened and not open to see the new thing God is doing through Jesus and those whose eyes, ears, and hearts are indeed open to God.[17]

So in these verses disciples are assured by Jesus that they are spiritually privileged people. God has chosen them to receive the revelation that God's *basileia* has drawn near in Jesus. Therefore, they should understand the parable Jesus has just told (vv. 3–9). But his next words to them, "Do you not understand this parable?" (v. 13) indicates uncertainty as to whether or not they have understood. If they do not understand this parable, then they are in the same position as those on the outside who cannot understand. None of the parables will be intelligible to them in that case. Verse 13 thus closes the passage begun at verse 10 by beginning to shift the focus from God's initiative to the response of the hearers: Authentic disciples will perceive the mystery. Julian of Norwich could have been explaining these verses when she told her followers in the fourteenth century, "The revelation is never sufficient; it is a grace and God takes all the initiative, but there must be human effort. The extraordinary does not dispense with the ordinary."[18]

Clearly, then, understanding is an authentic response to God's revelation. But how do disciples understand a mystery? Mark's Jesus graciously follows his challenge to his disciples in verse 13 with an interpretation of the sower parable (vv. 14–20) that focuses on responses to the word of God. His interpretation answers the question about how disciples may attain understanding.

Verses 14–20:
The Responses

Mark's editing activity has made the interpretation of the sower parable the hinge on which the whole discourse turns (see the outline, above). Its placement alerts us to give these words special attention.

The interpretation reveals immediately what the seed that the sower planted is: "The sower sows the word" (v. 14). There are four types of soils (hearers of the word) into which the seed falls, but for Mark's Jesus there are really only two groups of hearers: those who hear the word and accept it and those who do not. The responses of potential disciples that cause the seed (word) to fail will demonstrate inauthentic responses to God's initiative of giving the word (4:11). The responses of potential disciples that cause the seed (word) to flourish reveal the authentic responses to God.

The inauthentic responses begin in verse 15 with Satan's opposition to the word. Satan is represented in the parable as birds that come and immediately eat the seed that was sown on the path (4:4). Though Mark's story has revealed that Jesus "binds the strong man" (3:27; strong man is a reference to Satan), the final overthrow of Satan will not occur until the consummation of God's *basileia*. Meanwhile Satan remains active as the evil that blocks the word. The reference to Satan taking away the word (4:15) implies that some people choose evil and are never open to hear Jesus' word at all, an obviously inauthentic response.

Among those who hear the word but whose response is nevertheless judged as inauthentic are those who immediately hear it with joy but have no root in themselves (v. 16). They are represented in the parable as seed sown on rocky ground where there is too little soil for roots (4:5). Rootlessness is a traditional image of instability or transitoriness. Rootless people "endure only for a while" (v. 17). The Greek word underlying this phrase is rare and has fostered translations such as "ephemeral," "capricious as the weather," or people "of a moment."[19] When persecution or tribulation arises because of the word, rootless people fall away. Perhaps they did not hear the word Jesus sowed as the very truth of God from which they cannot turn no matter the cost. Perhaps they joined Jesus' movement only for what they could gain for themselves—forgiveness, access to God's power, places of honor in God's new order—so that when their participation began to cost them instead, they quit. The Greek word for "fall away" actually means "to snare" or "to set a trap for." The idea is that when these people are persecuted they are trapped because their faith is so feeble.[20]

The inauthentic responses, then, are having a rootless faith and, as a result of such weak faith, falling away in the face of persecution on account of the word. By implication, deep roots of faith are needed to endure through persecution to eternity. Thus the authentic responses would be to allow the word to grow roots deep within one's heart[21] and, on the strength of such roots, to persevere, even through persecution, to the end.

The thorny soil (4:7) reveals those who have heard the word but who allow the anxiety of the times, the delight in riches, and the lust for other things to enter in and choke the word (vv. 18–19). The implication is that the word has not been given the choice "soil" in the heart necessary to gain a permanent place. Instead, a heart full of anxiety and lust for riches and other things produces "thorns" that easily choke the word to death. Mark's Jesus underlines here the specific corruption of affluence and all that goes with it (status, position, power, and more).[22] Fruitlessness is the pathetic result of these inauthentic responses to the word that God gives. The authentic response would be devotion to the word of God that gives it the best and greatest part of the heart and leaves anxiety and lust for wealth and other things rootless and fruitless.

The authentic response, the opposite of fruitlessness, is shown in the good soil (4:8, 20), which represents those hearers who do more than hear the word Jesus sows and let it go for one reason or another. These hear and accept the word, allowing it to penetrate right into their hearts. They keep it and cleave to it, understanding it as the very truth of God and reorienting their lives according to it.[23] As a result, they bear an extravagant amount of fruit—thirty, sixty, a hundredfold, when a ten-to-one return on seed was considered a bumper crop![24] The Hebrew Bible understood such fruit to be justice and righteousness (see Isa. 5:7). These hearers have no desire to attend to riches or other things and are able to withstand persecution to the end. The Greek verbs in the verse emphasize the continual faithful and fruitful—that is, just and righteous—response of these hearers.[25] This response is the one authentic disciples will make to God who is sowing the mystery of God's *basileia* through Jesus.

Verses 21–25:
Further Responses

The completion of the material addressed to the disciples comes in verses 21–25. We found that verses 11–13 treated God's revealing and electing initiatives that enable true disciples to understand Jesus' parables. Verses 14–20 followed and focused on the responses that must be made by the ones chosen to receive the word of God. The paradox—God's revealing and electing activity (vv. 11–13) juxtaposed with the disciples' responsibility (vv. 14–20)—is held in tension rather than resolved. That tension is continued in verses 21–25.

Verse 21 presents the parable of the lamp: "Does a lamp come in so that it may be placed under a bushel basket or under the bed? Does it not come in so that it may be placed on a lampstand?" This parable suggests that the mystery of God's *basileia* is destined to be revealed. Verse 22 follows by insisting that nothing is hidden "but so that it may be revealed." In other words, the lamp may indeed be (unexpectedly) hidden, but it is hidden so that it may be revealed by the act of hiding it. If Jesus' parables indeed invite hearers into the story and trick them into seeing through it to a truer story behind the story, then they enable hearers to experience the mystery of God's *basileia* precisely because of their parabolic nature. The mystery is concealed in parables in order that it may come to light.[26] But it will do so only for those who hear and accept the word as in 4:20. So, Mark's Jesus concludes these words with the challenge: "If anyone has ears to hear, let her or him hear!" (v. 23).

Jesus then follows with a command in verse 24 that adds to the challenge to hear: "See what you hear!" We intuit immediately that he must not mean ordinary seeing and hearing. How can persons actually see what they hear (the literal translation of the Greek)? This command is itself parabolic. It calls for seeing which is more than "looking at" something on its surface. This type of seeing is a metaphor for understanding, grasping the significance, perceiving what is genuine (the truer story behind the story). Later in Mark's story the same type of seeing and hearing is stressed. At 8:15 Jesus warns his disciples, "Look, see the leaven of the Pharisees and the leaven of Herod." Though leaven had become a metaphor for the evil inclination of humankind,[27] the disciples "see" only surface things. They think Jesus is concerned because they have forgotten to bring bread (8:16). Their blindness prompts a sharp retort from Jesus: "Why do you discuss that you have no bread? Do you not yet perceive or understand? Are your hearts hardened? *Having eyes do you not see and having ears do you not hear?*" (8:17–18, emphasis mine). Then Jesus reminds them of the feeding miracles (6:33–44; 8:19–20) as if to assure them of his ability to care for their physical (surface) needs. They must attend to their "seeing and hearing." Still later Jesus himself practices his teaching when he "sees" that the scribe who said that loving God and others is much more than all whole burnt offerings and sacrifices has "answered well" (12:33–34). Such seeing is akin to the understanding called for in 4:13 and is an authentic response to God who reveals the mystery of God's *basileia*.

The phrases that follow—"In what measure you measure it will be measured to you and will be given to you" (v. 24b); "For whoever has, more will be given to him or her; but the one who has not, even what he or she has will be taken away" (v. 25)—show the consequences of responding authentically or not to the word that God gives. For those who hear and grasp the word and have eyes to see the mystery of God (the truer story behind the story), there will always be more of God to know, understand, appreciate, worship. But those who see only the surface have no true vision and are completely unable to see the presence of the *basileia* of God as it is revealed through Jesus in Mark's story.

The Seed Parables: What They Add

The conclusion to this discourse (v. 34) implies that Mark knew other parables of Jesus but selected only a few examples whose central point is the sowing of the word, or God's revelation. Together they form a group of teachings united by both theme (sowing the seed/word) and their place in the structure of the discourse (the B and B' parts of the parallel structure). Since the parables frame the teachings in the center of the discourse, we expect them to lend support to the teachings there.

The Sower Parable (4:3–9)

In the first parable there is again strong emphasis on hearing. The parable is introduced with the command, "Listen!" (v. 3), and concludes with the challenge, "Let the one having ears to hear hear!" (v. 9). These words are exhortations, this time to all the crowd around Jesus, to the same true hearing we saw in 4:20, 23–24. The ones having ears to hear the truer story behind the story can so listen to Jesus that they actually "see" the presence of the *basileia* of God in his words, works, and destiny, though surface appearances might suggest otherwise (How could God be present in a peasant carpenter from Galilee?). Indeed, the parable is about deceptive appearances. In the stagnant, subsistence economy of Jesus' hearers, failure of three-fourths of the seed would appear to be utter disaster. Instead, the one-fourth of the seed that fell on good soil (those who hear the word and accept it, 4:20) produced thirty, sixty, a hundredfold when tenfold would have been a bumper crop. Instead of failure, there is an extravagant harvest. Things are not always what they appear to be. Those who hear and see as Jesus called them to do are able to grasp this truth. The authentic response to Jesus' parables is to hear (and see) in this way.

The Seed Growing on Its Own (4:26–29) and the Mustard Seed (4:30–32)

After Mark's Jesus told his disciples that the mystery of God's *basileia* has been given to them, and after he instructed them how they should and should not respond to this revelation, he tells his "kingdom parables." Appropriately, there is an air of mystery about each of them.

The middle of the parable of the seed growing on its own, verses 27–28, contains two interpretive asides that are the primary pointers to the parable's meaning. The first of these is that the sower did not know how the seed grew (v. 27). The second is the note that the earth produced "of itself," a phrase that is from a single Greek word that can be expressed as "without recognizable cause" and even as "worked by God."[28] The mystery of growth is independent of human effort and happens by the power of God alone. The development from seed to harvest is God's deed, God's wonder. The sower did not, could not, need not cause the seed to grow. The principal interest is assigned to the mysterious growth of the seed that has been sown.

The mustard seed story is a contrast parable. Its meaning lies in the contrast between the smallest seed and the greatest shrub with the realization that the latter grew from the former. But it is not just any shrub. The smallest seed produces a shrub that puts forth branches so big that the birds make nests in its shade. The healthy plant symbolizes the life-giving power of God's *basileia*.[29]

A sense of improbability pervades these parables. A harvest comes from seed though humans do not know how; the smallest seed becomes a tremendous bush. Again, things are not what they appear to be. Mark's Jesus claims that God's *basileia* is experienced as being like that—improbable, surprising, unexpected. As kingdom parables, these two affirm the mystery (4:10–11) as it has been interpreted here: God's *basileia* has drawn near in the mission of Jesus of Nazareth. At the moment it is hidden, and may even appear to be absent. But it is here and available. Furthermore, its coming in glory is irresistible, certain, and independent of human effort. Mark believed that God decided to launch God's *basileia* through the ministry of Jesus, and God is doing so. No one need worry about its coming, nor should anyone try to force its culmination. Instead disciples should trust and "see" that God is surely at work. In the end God's *basileia* will bear its ripe fruit. The nations will find their definitive rest within its shade. The parables portray God's ultimate fulfillment even in the midst of what appears to be an unpromising beginning. They call Jesus' hearers to a radical faith in God that looks beyond what it sees to that for which it hopes[30] (the truer story behind the story). Such faith is an authentic response to God who reveals the mystery of God's *basileia*.

Summary of Mark 4:1–34

In this discourse Mark's Jesus presents God as one who gives revelation about the mystery of God's *basileia* to those who have been called to hear it. The mystery is that God has taken the initiative to launch God's *basileia* through the mission of Jesus of Nazareth. As a result of God's initiatives, disciples who have been given the revelation are challenged to see and hear beyond surface appearances to the truer story behind the story. How valuable could such seeing and hearing be today in our "style over substance" culture?

Authentic disciples see and hear the presence of God's *basileia* in Jesus' words and actions. They accept God's word sowed by Jesus as though seeds were being planted deeply into their hearts and nurtured there. Such seeing and hearing of Jesus' word produces a radical faith that enables followers to commit themselves to their belief that God's *basileia* has drawn near in the mission of Jesus though at present it is hidden from ordinary sight. People with such faith believe that God's *basileia* will culminate in glorious power despite its humble beginnings because God's word says so. So they endure persecution on account of the word and are not seduced by anxiety or lust for riches or other things. They trust God, believing that God is at work and will bring fulfillment as promised. Their lives bear an extravagant harvest of the fruits of justice and righteousness. These are authentic responses to God's initiative. They are the ones toward which Mark wants members of his community to grow.

The inauthentic responses Mark wants his community to leave behind begin with surface hearing of Jesus' word that results in neither seeing nor accepting the truer story of God hidden beyond the surface.

The heart is too full of the anxiety of the times and lust for riches and other things to give full attention to Jesus' word or have room for faith's deep roots. Though there might be initial enthusiasm for the word, it is a rootless enthusiasm concerned only with what can be gained which produces transitoriness and instability. It does not see God at work through Jesus. It does not trust God to fulfill God's *basileia*. It falters before persecution on account of the word. It is choked by the lusts of the heart. The faithlessness of the inauthentic responses results in fruitlessness: no justice, no righteousness. Those who so respond never "see" that the *basileia* of God, presently hidden in Jesus, has drawn near to them.

Mark 7:1–23

Mark's second major presentation of Jesus' teaching (7:1–23) occurs just as Jesus is beginning to take his ministry beyond Galilee (note 6:45, 53; 7:24). Perhaps Mark placed this conflict story after Jesus fed the five thousand and walked on the water (6:30–56), stories that emphasize Jesus' success, because he would never leave his readers long without a reminder of the opposition Jesus aroused. Furthermore, Mark likely placed this story before the incident with the Syrophoenician woman so that its new definition of purity would prepare readers to accept her right to share the bread of Israel's children (7:24–30).[31] In our study of miracles we will examine her story more closely. Meanwhile we are occupied with Jesus' teaching on purity which was prompted by a controversy over the validity of the religion practiced by the scribes and Pharisees. Thus this incident can tell us much about Mark's spirituality.

The composite nature of this section of the Gospel[32] suggests that Mark is responsible for bringing together various sayings of Jesus about the religious leaders and their rules of ritual cleanness. The result of his editorial work is a tightly structured story with a thematic unity. The following outline of the passage will guide our study:

A. Introduction and question (verses 1–5)
    1. Pharisees and scribes see the disciples' omission: 1–2
    2. Markan explanation and generalization: 3–4
    3. double question: 5
        a. regarding tradition: 5b
        b. regarding eating with unclean hands: 5c

    B. Jesus' answer (verses 6–23)
        1. regarding tradition: 6–13
            a. counterattack (Isaiah text): 6–8
            b. illustration (Corban practice): 9–13
        2. regarding defilement: 14–23
            a. public proclamation: 14–15
            b. private explanation: 17–23.[33]

God's Initiatives

The initiatives of God to which the participants in this story must respond are implied by two sets of competing responses. First, there is a contrast between obedience to the commands of God recorded in the Hebrew Scriptures and adherence to human traditions created by the religious elders. Second, there is a contrast between ritual purity and purity of heart. Since the call to purity is part of scripture, the two sets of responses are related to each other and revolve around scripture. Thus the initiatives of God at issue in this passage are God's gift of scripture and God's call to purity contained in scripture.

The Responses

The first two verses of the passage introduce the conflict of the story. Some Pharisees and scribes who had come from Jerusalem[34] saw Jesus' disciples eating with defiled or unwashed hands (i.e., "common" or "secular" hands as opposed to "holy" and "set apart for God," v. 2). Mark, in an editorial aside, explained that the rule insisting on hand-washing before eating came from the tradition of the elders (v. 3), that is, the oral tradition the Pharisees considered as binding as the written law. Scripture offered at best some support for the practice. Thus the disciples were violating human traditions, not scripture. Verse 4, continuing Mark's explanation, then presents details of general Jewish traditions of ritual purification such as the washing of cups, pots, and bronze vessels. Scholars often note that these explanations would have been needed if Mark's readers included Gentiles. But verses 3–4 also serve a theological necessity in this story. They widen the purity issue beyond clean hands and prepare the way for the Pharisees' double question in verse 5.[35]

Their question ends where the conflict began: Why do Jesus' disciples eat without ritually cleaning their hands (v. 5c)? The second set of competing responses is at issue—ritual purity versus purity of heart.

But this specific charge is really a peg for the wider issue of obeying scripture versus adhering to human traditions which is raised by the beginning of the question: Why do Jesus' disciples not conform their lives to the tradition of the elders (v. 5b)? The question sets the stage for Mark's Jesus to tell us which of these sets of competing responses is authentic and which is not.

Jesus addresses the wider issue first. He begins, appropriately enough, with a quote from scripture (vv. 6–7). The Septuagint reading of Isaiah 29:13, "in vain do they worship me, teaching doctrines and teachings of human beings," has been interpreted here to read, "teaching human commandments as doctrines" (v. 7).[36] Jesus uses this interpretation of Isaiah to describe the devotion of the religious leaders to merely human ordinances over the commandments of God in scripture. For this devotion Jesus called them "hypocrites" (v. 6). The name-calling clearly indicates the inauthenticity of this response to God's gift of scripture. Verse 8 then gives Jesus' commentary or midrash on the Isaiah passage: "Having left the commandment of God you hold fast to human traditions." The force of the midrash is that to "honor God with the lips" means to uphold the traditions of mere human beings. Rejection of the divine commandments indicates a heart which is "far from God." What God commands in scripture and what human beings ordain are set in radical opposition to one another. To choose to uphold the latter at the expense of the former is the inauthentic response in Mark. Here we see the organizing form for Markan spirituality set in sharp relief: the Way of the Lord versus the Way of Humanity.

Then Jesus gives an example to illustrate his charge against the religious leaders (vv. 9–13). Using scripture again, he begins, "Moses said . . ." (v. 10) and then follows with a double quotation from Exodus 20:12 ("Honor your father and your mother") and 21:17 ("Let the one speaking evil of father or mother surely die"). His choice of scripture is intended to underline the importance the written law attached to one's duty to one's parents. He then continued, "But *you* say if a man says to his mother or father, 'Whatever you would have received from me is Corban, which is a gift,' you no longer allow him to do anything for his father or mother" (vv. 11–12). The force of the pronoun "you" in Greek is emphatic and intentionally provocative since it contrasts with "Moses said" in verse 10. It shows that the elders in their tradition, not God, judged positively the decision to evade scriptural obligations to dependent parents by naming earnings as Corban, that is, making it a gift to the Temple. It is surely no coincidence that the economy of the Temple sucked the life out of the poorest and most vulnerable people, such as the elderly, to sustain the lifestyle of the Jerusalem religious establishment, as we will see when 11:12–25 is examined. Jesus declares that such a judgment against dependent parents made the word of God void (v. 13a). Furthermore, this is but one example of many ways these religious leaders annul God's commandment (v. 13b).

This illustration goes beyond Jesus' first accusation in verses 6–8 where he charged that they neglected God's commands. In the Corban example he spoke of violating God's commands to keep the human traditions. Both are inauthentic responses to God who has gifted us with scripture. These inauthentic responses demonstrate that the authentic responses are devotion to scripture and obedience to God's commands in scripture. These authentic responses are surely no surprise to us. Holy Scripture was one of the principal institutions of first-century Judaism and Jewish spirituality. The Hebrew Scriptures were also considered the revelation of God by the first Christians. Every word of the sacred text was thought to be pregnant with divine meaning. It served as the pure and perennial source of the spiritual life of first-century Christians and Jews.[37] It continues to do so for many contemporary Christians.

This high view of scripture is exhibited by Jesus throughout Mark. In 12:36 Mark's Jesus refers to the psalms of David as inspired by the Holy Spirit. If he considered the psalms to be divinely inspired, then he would have surely thought of the most sacred part of the Hebrew Scriptures—the law—as divinely inspired.[38] Indeed, Mark recorded two places where Jesus used the law positively: the story of the rich man (10:17–22), and in answer to the question regarding the greatest commandment (12:28–34). But Mark also showed Jesus turning to scripture for support when literal exegesis was not employed: he used the story of David and the shewbread as precedent for plucking grain on the Sabbath (2:23–28), quoted Isaiah and Jeremiah as revealing the true purpose of the Temple when he drove out the money changers (11:17), cited Exodus 3:6 to prove the reality of the resurrection (12:24–27), and claimed that the Sadducees were wrong about the resurrection because they did not know the scriptures (12:24). Finally, Mark's Jesus expected that the prophecies of scripture would be fulfilled. He declared that Elijah had come, meaning John the Baptist, and had been treated "just as it has been written of him" (9:13). When

captured in Gethsemane, he resigned himself to the violence surrounding him so that the scriptures "might be fulfilled" (14:49). Jesus'
devotion to scripture is obvious and indicates an authentic response to
this gift from God.

Yet there is another side to Jesus' attitude toward scripture. In the
second part of the story in 7:1–23 he set aside a portion of the Mosaic
law—the dietary laws (Lev. 11—15, Deut. 14)—with the simple declaration that what goes into a person cannot defile since it enters the
stomach, not the heart (vv. 18–19a). Human beings are, among other
things, moral and spiritual beings. Food, however, passes only through
the body. Thus, all foods are clean (v. 19c). The dietary laws in scripture are no longer binding. Mark's Jesus has just voided the word of
God, the very charge he leveled at his opponents!

There are other times in Mark's Gospel when Jesus is opposed to
the literal text of scripture in much the same way as in 7:18–19. He
challenged the priority of the Sabbath laws with his claim to be "lord
also of the sabbath" (2:28) and became angry at the religious leaders
when they would have used the Sabbath laws to prevent a man's healing (3:1–6). He abrogated Moses' prescription for divorce by his own
authority (10:4–9). He seems to have been indifferent to the literal text
of scripture when it ran counter to his understanding of God's will,
which was formulated in terms that gave the right of way in cases of
conflict to the well-being of persons.[39] The greatest commandment
episode (12:28–34) shows the priority of human well-being clearly.
When asked about the greatest commandment, Mark's Jesus responded by quoting two commandments from scripture that make
loving God and neighbor the highest commands. God's high concern
for human beings is evident: loving others ranks alongside loving God.
Literal adherence to scripture does not take priority over loving others, especially others who are in need. Instead, we may infer from
Jesus' teachings that an authentic response to God's gift of scripture is
to allow it to challenge us to love God and others more fully.

From Mark's Jesus, then, we learn to respect and devote ourselves
to scripture. We see him being sharply critical of those who make
God's word void—this is an inauthentic response to God's gift of
scripture. Nevertheless, scripture must not be used to oppress or devalue people. This response too is an inauthentic one to God's word.
When the literal text of scripture could be used to allow such an inauthentic response, Jesus does not hesitate to set the text aside. His attitude toward scripture is in touch with God's will, one aspect of

which is expressed in the command to love God and love others. Respect and devotion toward and use in loving God and others are all authentic responses to God's gift of Holy Scripture.

We may ask at this point: Why must the food laws go? How were they used to oppress people? We turn back to 7:14 where the story shifts to Jesus' response to his disciples eating with defiled hands. He called the people to him as he answered. He commanded them to "hear and understand," so that we are made aware again that perceiving the truth of his words is an authentic response to what God is revealing through Christ. The content of Jesus' teaching moves now from scripture itself to what scripture says about being clean (set apart) for God.

The first part of the "parable" Jesus speaks here states unequivocally that food is unable to make a person unclean ("nothing that is outside a person by going in is able to defile that person," v. 15a). The second part then discloses what is able to cause defilement ("but the things which come out from a person are what defile that person," v. 15b). The antithesis in the two lines is changed from a contrast between material and material thing (food versus bodily waste, v. 15a) to a contrast between material and spiritual thing (food versus spiritual defilement, v. 15b).[40] So, verse 15 "spiritualizes" the idea of purity and calls for people to be clean in their inner selves.

After making his pronouncement, Jesus leaves the crowd and goes into a house where his disciples ask him about the parable (v. 17). His question to them in response, "Are *you* [emphatic pronoun] also without understanding?" (v. 18a), brings to mind his urging them "to see" in 4:13, 24–25. As in Mark 4, the disciples' question gives Jesus a chance for a detailed explanation of his parable: food cannot defile a person because it enters the stomach, not the heart (v. 19). In verse 20 he repeats the thought of verse 15b: "What comes out of a person is what defiles that person." The heart is no mere romantic symbol, but refers, according to Semitic thinking, to the personal center of the person where thoughts are conceived, decisions made.[41] Only what comes from within this personal center can defile a person according to Jesus. The authentic response to God's call in scripture to purity or holiness is, according to Jesus in Mark, a matter of a clean heart that is close to God.

The disciples' difficulty in understanding Jesus' parable is doubtless due to their having been reared on a different concept of purity that permeated their culture and that their religious leaders espoused. This view of purity is illustrated by the Temple's structure. The most Holy Place (the Holy of Holies), into which only the high priest could go once a year, was placed within an inner court into which only priests could go, which was placed within a court into which only appropriate Jewish men could go, which was followed by a court into which only appropriate Jewish women could go, which was surrounded by an open, walled-in courtyard where Gentiles were finally allowed. As is clear, whether or not a person was allowed near the Holy Place, consigned to the courtyard, or able to venture somewhere in between was determined solely by birth (ethnicity, gender, family, illegitimacy, birth defects).[42] The attitude reflected in the Temple structure is, "Keep the rabble far from the center, and the center cannot be defiled." The religious leaders built similar "fences" around the law, putting layer upon layer of interpretation around it down to the smallest details so that people could not possibly break (and defile) it. Thus when they turned to individual purity, they would be concerned with pots, pans, food, and hands. They were reflecting their belief that if the outside is kept clean, then nothing unclean can enter and defile the center. A religion with such a view of purity is bound to stress externals, boundaries, and surfaces, to give greatest importance to activity over attitude, to performance over intention, and finally, to holiness over compassion.[43] Consequently, women, Gentiles, those with skin diseases, persons whose occupations would not allow them to do ritual washings or always eat kosher were considered less pure, were devalued by this definition of purity and denied full participation in the community of God's people.[44]

We have already seen, however, that Mark's Jesus called followers to look beneath the surface to the truer story there. We should not be surprised, then, that he looked beneath the externals and surfaces to a person's heart for her or his purity. Thus he claimed there was no need for concern over ritual washings and kosher food since these could not reach a person's heart. Throughout the Second Gospel, Jesus demonstrated his understanding of true purity. In 1:41 he touched a leper as he healed him. Since a leper was ritually unclean, touching him made Jesus "unclean" (Lev. 13:46). But Jesus did not let that rule stop him from reaching out to him and restoring him to God's people (1:44). Similarly, he came in contact with a woman who had had a flow of blood for twelve years (5:25) and called her "daughter" (5:34), and touched the dead body of Jairus's daughter (5:38). Both actions would make him unclean (Lev. 15:19–27; Num. 19:11–14). Both times he cared more for people than for rules. His God did not demand a purity that necessitated withdrawal from ordinary, hurting human beings. When Mark's Jesus came in contact with suffering and need he felt he could alleviate, he freely ran the risk of ceremonial defilement in order to end people's pain and isolation.[45] We have already noted that he named loving God and others the two greatest commandments. The scribe who originally asked him about the greatest commandment responded to Jesus' answer by agreeing that love of God and others is "greater than all the whole burnt offerings and sacrifices" (12:33). Jesus told him, "You are not far from the *basileia* of God" (12:34). Thus with his words in Mark 7 and his actions throughout Mark's story, Jesus subverted the whole concept of external purity held by so many ancient religions, including that of the Jewish religious leaders,[46] thereby indicating its inauthenticity. He replaced that concept with a call to purity of heart that turns one's whole being toward God and God's will, thus indicating the authenticity of this response.

Jesus then reiterated his call by listing the causes of true defilement (7:21–22). The list includes six specific acts (evil thoughts, sexual immorality, theft, murder, adultery, and lust of possession) and seven vices (malice, deceit, fornication, envy, slander, arrogance, and folly).[47] All these acts and vices hurt and devalue other people. They are obviously inauthentic responses to God. Verse 23 concludes the discussion by noting that these evil things come from within and are what defile a person. Thus Mark's Jesus has taught that persons who are ritually pure but whose hearts cause them to oppress or devalue others are responding inauthentically to God's call to be holy. Persons who are ritually unclean but who love God and others have clean, holy hearts and are responding authentically to God's call to be holy. Thus a woman could be more holy than a man, a Gentile more holy than a Jew, a leper more holy than a priest. Think of the implications for today in our increasingly multicultural world. No wonder Mark called this teaching of Jesus a parable—certainly it is world-subverting discourse!

Finally, we can observe that, in addition to promoting a lack of compassion for others, compliance with external rituals is visible and measurable. It codifies God's will so that "success" before God is visible and measurable. Ritual purity may serve the status and honor of the ones observing them, instead of serving God, thus enabling them to justify themselves before God and others.[48] Mark has drawn a sharp contrast between Jesus' lack of concern for purity regulations when he could help others and his enemies' excessive concern for complying with elaborate purity rituals, many of them created by human traditions, for the purpose of satisfying their desire for status and honor. These religious leaders were not really seeking God but their interests.

Summary of Mark 7:1–23

God's initiatives in this story were discovered to be the gift of scripture and, in particular, God's call in scripture to be holy or pure before God.

Inauthentic responses to these initiatives begin with devotion to human traditions over scripture. Such devotion is evident in the religious leaders' willingness to abandon and even reject scripture in order to observe their human traditions. These kinds of human traditions are themselves inauthentic because they foster, according to Mark's story, an external purity that is concerned for externals, surfaces, and boundaries (ritual washings, gender, race, physical limitations, eating kosher). Further, an external purity can boost a person's sense of privilege before God and over others. This type of purity turns the heart away from God and others, and turns it toward oneself and one's group. These inauthentic responses suggest a profound question for the church today: In what ways are we still practicing an external view of purity?

Interestingly, those who adhered to an external purity insisted on holding to a literal interpretation of scripture when it served their tradition and sense of importance to do so. An example of this use of scripture is the food laws of Leviticus and Deuteronomy. Since it was nearly impossible for most of the population to maintain the kosher practices, insisting on them enabled the religious leaders to present themselves as more pure, more holy than the common people. Their hypocrisy with regard to scripture highlights their inauthentic response to this initiative of God. Again, a significant question for the contemporary church is prompted by this inauthentic response: How do our personal interests and conveniences influence our adherence to God's commands in scripture?

Finally, we note the list of acts and vices Mark's Jesus gives at the end of his teaching here. Since he tells us that these are the things that cause true defilement, we know that evil thoughts, sexual immorality, theft, murder, adultery, lust of possession, malice, deceit, fornication, envy, slander, arrogance, and folly are inauthentic responses to God who calls us to be holy.

The authentic responses to God's initiatives begin with devotion toward and respect for scripture as practiced by Mark's Jesus. He insisted that scripture's commands should never be set aside to suit one's own traditions or concerns. But this devotion does not involve adherence to the literal meaning of the text of scripture when that adherence would allow persons to be oppressed or devalued. Thus scripture should not be used to exalt oneself or one's group by allowing one to claim purity before God because of ritual or to devalue others by judging them unclean and common because they were born Gentile or female, ate the wrong foods with dirty hands, or for any other reason. According to Mark's Jesus, scripture should aid persons in obeying God's will, a major aspect of which is expressed in the two most important commandments: love God and love others as oneself.

Indeed, a disciple who is authentically pure in Mark has a heart set apart for God, a heart that is close to God. Her or his holiness is revealed in what comes forth from within. What does not come forth from a clean heart are acts and vices that oppress and devalue other people. Thus the authentic response to God's gift of scripture and its call to be holy or pure before God is a combination of devotion to scripture and a heart that is set apart for God, loves God, and loves and values others as Jesus did.

Chapter 3

Responding to the God of Life, Inclusiveness, Power, and Nearness

In Mark, Jesus taught about the way of the Lord not only with his words but also by the actions he took throughout his ministry. In Mark's story, Jesus' parabolic words and his miracles blend into one so that the miracles also reveal the God-willed significance of Jesus' mission. For those who understand the miracles, as for those who understand the parables, they are signs of God's initiative to intersect the visible, material world and reach out to God's people. They are important not so much for their outward form as for their spiritual significance as works of God.[1]

Jesus' miracles are part of the proclamation of the *basileia* of God in Mark. They are not proofs that Jesus is from God, nor are they wonders at which to marvel. They are signs of the presence of God's grace. They may even be viewed as outward and sacramental signs of a dawning but not yet fully disclosed *basileia* of God.[2] Since disease among human beings and chaos in the world were understood as parts of the disobedience of creation against its Creator and one means by which Satan held creation in bondage, miracles of healing and exorcism meant that God's plan for the redress of humanity was being activated.[3] Thus the miracles disclose more than the fact of the inbreaking of God's *basileia*. They also reveal the manner in which the *basileia* comes. Where God's realm spreads there is a marvelous breakthrough in the struggle against oppressive restrictions on human life.[4] Through the transforming event of the miracle, people are freed from bondage and made whole.

The first miracle follows Mark's introduction of Jesus (1:9–15). Jesus of Nazareth was endowed with the Spirit of God and affirmed as God's own—an intersection of the spirit and material worlds—at his baptism (vv. 9–11). In the power of the Spirit he set out to wrest Satan's dominion away (vv. 12–13). He proclaimed the inbreaking of

God's *basileia* and, thus, that people could repent, that is, reorient their lives according to the message of the Gospel (vv. 14–15). Then, in the power of God's Spirit Jesus challenged Satan by exorcising a demon in a synagogue in his first miracle (1:21–28). Mark's readers are meant to see in these beginnings that Jesus brings God's *basileia* near to ordinary human beings by the power of God's Spirit. Thus the miracles of Mark's Jesus are excellent vehicles for examining the experience of God reflected in Mark's Gospel.

The miracles also offer excellent opportunities to examine persons' responses to these experiences of God, for clearly the miracles can be misunderstood. The Gospel is full of people who are changed positively by Jesus' God-given power. There are also people, however, who are blind to the miracles—not to the extent or wonder of them, but to their true meaning. In this chapter we are seeking understanding of the experiences of God and the responses to these in the miracle stories in the first half of Mark's Gospel (3:1–6; 4:35–41; 7:24–30).

Mark 3:1–6

The story in Mark 3:1–6 concludes a cycle of five conflict stories begun at 2:1. Just prior, at 1:45, Jesus is in the country unable to enter towns openly because of his popularity among the peasants of Galilee. The verses that follow this cycle, 3:7–12, also stress Jesus' popularity. By framing the conflict cycle with stories emphasizing Jesus' popularity among the common people, Mark has heightened the sense of hostility that is building between Jesus and the religious leaders in 2:1–3:6.

The first four conflicts in the cycle involve Jesus forgiving sins (2:1–12), his eating with sinners (vv. 15–17), the question of fasting (vv. 18–22), and harvesting grain on the Sabbath (vv. 23–28). The climax of the cycle comes in the story examined here, the healing of the man with the withered hand (3:1–6). Since the healing occurs on the Sabbath, it continues the Sabbath debate begun with the grain harvesting in the fourth story. In the first Sabbath conflict Jesus claimed to be Lord of the Sabbath. In this climactic story of the cycle he will demonstrate this lordship.[5]

God's Initiative

Jesus entered the synagogue and discovered a man with a dried-up or withered hand (3:1). The Greek verb often translated "withered" is used in 4:6 and 11:21 to indicate plants that have withered and died. Thus there is a sense of lifelessness about this word. The man's hand is not just lacking; it is lifeless. The use of this verb, then, reveals a first nuance cast on the miracle God will do through Jesus in this story. In 3:5 when Jesus restores the man's hand, he restores life to the hand. The unexpected use of resurrection language in 3:3 ("rise into the middle"[6])and Jesus' question in 3:4 add to the theme of life in the story. Thus the initiative of God in this story is the granting of God's power through Jesus for the restoration or resurrection of life.

A second nuance cast on the miracle of God in this story involves the when of its occurrence: Jesus unleashes God's life-restoring power on the *Sabbath*. As will be shown in what follows, Jesus' action not only restores a man's hand, it also restores God's intent for the Sabbath as a day of joy, health, and celebration. Taken together, the two nuances Mark casts on this miracle enable us to share Mark's experience of God as the restorer of God's good gifts and, thus, as a God full of *life*.

The Responses

A man with a withered or lifeless hand would immediately be noticed in the synagogue when the congregation stood for prayer and raised their hands to shoulder height, palms upward.[7] So "they" watched Jesus intently to see if he would heal this man on the Sabbath so that they could accuse him (v. 2). The Greek verb for "watch" implies a sense of hostility or of lying in wait.[8] In verse 6 we learn that "they" are the Pharisees. Verse 6 also reveals how the Pharisees respond to the miracle that they watch: They plot with the Herodians to murder Jesus. Both the reference to the motivation of Jesus' opposition in verse 2 ("so that they might accuse him") and all of verse 6 (the plot against Jesus) are considered explanations inserted by Mark into the story.[9] By means of these insertions Mark has emphasized that the religious leaders' response is the complete antithesis of God's initiative. While God is restoring life through Jesus, the religious leaders are plotting to take Jesus' life from him. We remember that murder is included in the list of actions in 7:21–22 that come from within a person's heart making him or her unclean. Not respecting life is an obviously inauthentic response to God's life-giving initiative through Jesus.

The religious leaders justified their death sentence against Jesus by their belief that he had violated the Sabbath. Their concern at the beginning of the story was not, "Can Jesus heal?" Everyone, including Jesus' opponents, takes his power to accomplish the miraculous for granted. Their question was whether or not he would heal on the Sabbath. Healing was considered an infringement of the character of the Sabbath because treatment of bodily suffering was viewed as work, as a creative contribution that conflicted with the purpose of the day of rest. A break from human activity was necessary because of the call to every Israelite to be pure or holy as God is holy. Holiness, however, could be difficult to combine with the activity of daily life and work, especially for peasants.[10] Hence a day was set aside to disconnect from work. Violation of the Sabbath, from the perspective of the religious leaders, could warrant the death penalty (cf. Ex. 31:14; 35:2; Jubilees).

The religious leaders' view of healing on the Sabbath corresponds closely to their view of plucking grain on the Sabbath in 2:23–28. In both stories they are advocates of not acting at all; any activity would be work that violates the day of rest. In the first story Jesus responds to their question as to why his disciples do what is not lawful on the Sabbath (plucking grain) by claiming that the Sabbath was made for humanity, not humanity for the Sabbath (2:27). As in 7:1–23, Mark's understanding of the place of the law amid God's special concern for human need stands forth here. Certainly the religious leaders' intent to use the Sabbath to block life-restoring healing in the second story is not an example of the Sabbath benefiting persons. Rather than viewing the law as a boon for humanity, they would use it to limit God's power to release a person from suffering. Their rigid interpretation of the Sabbath as a law against activity that was to be obeyed regardless of human cost contradicted God's concern for humans in need, God's gift of the Sabbath for the good of humanity, and Jesus' release of God's power on behalf of suffering humanity. Their view of Sabbath is, therefore, an inauthentic response to the compassionate God of life.

Mark tells his readers that the religious leaders' hearts were hard (3:5). This condition prevents the perception of all miracles of God, is no longer moved by need, and arms itself against any compassion with correct dogma, laws, or ethical rules.[11] Just as the religious leaders used their human traditions about purity to declare some persons unclean and keep them in "their place" in Mark 7, so they would use their view of law to "protect" the Sabbath from any work even though that meant maintaining a man's suffering, keeping him in Satan's death grip, and limiting God's power to restore life. Jesus is angry at them, grieved at their hard hearts (3:5). His grief and anger indicate the inauthenticity of these responses that derive from their hard, compassionless hearts.

What does Jesus expect instead of their view of the Sabbath and their hard hearts? The answer lies in the question he raises. Telling the man to "rise into the middle [i.e., the middle of the assembly]" (3:3), he asks, "Is it lawful on the sabbath to do good or to do evil, to save life or to kill it?" (v. 4). He does not debate whether or not healing is "work." To have done so would have been to accept their understanding of Sabbath with a view to refining what fit within their interpretation of the law. But he does not refine their understanding. As with the purity laws in 7:1–23, Jesus subverts their view. He does so by means of the two pairs of alternative actions he poses in his question. His question insists that the day of rest does not call for doing nothing when persons are in need. Instead, when faced with human need, people of God must choose between doing good and saving life or doing evil and killing life. When good ought to be done, there is no neutral ground.[12] Not acting is not an authentic option. In such situations, not to do good is to do evil. Jesus insists that the Sabbath rest is not an excuse for doing nothing when good could be done and lives could be saved.

Nor should it be! By the time of Jesus the Sabbath had taken on meaning beyond the obligatory rest. It had become suggestive to many of the rhythm of life shared by Yahweh and Israel wherein the seventh day marks completion. From these views rose a sense that the Sabbath's character was joyous and meant satisfaction. Later Jewish eschatology took advantage of the Sabbath's joyful character and pictured the time of salvation, the Age to Come, as among other things an extended Sabbath Day. By this tradition, then, the Sabbath was a fine day for Jesus to choose to do good and extend the *basileia* of God by freeing a person from Satan's domain and restoring life. To heal someone on the Sabbath would show that something of what the Sabbath had promised in the eschatological expectations of the Jewish people was being realized in Jesus' words and actions now.[13] The *basileia* of God has indeed drawn near! Thus Jesus not only sought to restore life to this man, he also wished to free the Sabbath from the restraints imposed on it by the religious leaders so that it "lives" among God's people as well.

The religious leaders did not answer Jesus' question (3:4). Their silence before the gauntlet Jesus has thrown down indicates their inability to counter his challenge and brings dishonor on them since, as religious leaders, they were supposed to understand the purpose of the law. In the midst of their silence, Jesus chooses the good and restores life to the man's hand (v. 5). In so doing he made the Sabbath a day filled with health, celebration, and the full possibilities of life in the *basileia* of God.[14] Through his release of the life-giving power of God, the Lord of the Sabbath (2:28) made the Sabbath serve humanity as it was meant to do (2:27). Thus observing the Sabbath in ways that meet human needs is an authentic response to God's gift of Sabbath rest. Furthermore, doing good and saving life are also authentic responses to God's gifts of both Sabbath rest and life-giving power. Doing evil and killing life are the obviously inauthentic responses. Doing nothing in the face of human need is equally inauthentic.

Summary of Mark 3:1–6

The initiatives of God in this story are revealed first in Jesus' release of God's power to "resurrect" a "lifeless" hand. The release of God's power on the Sabbath also had the effect of freeing that day—this part of the law—from the deadening restrictions imposed on it by the religious leaders and restoring it to what God had intended. Thus, God is experienced in this story as the compassionate God of *life*. God gives gifts to benefit humanity and acts to restore the gifts to that intent when people abuse them. God's life-granting power is shown to be stronger than Satan's death grip. Furthermore, God's compassion results in the release of that power on behalf of those who suffer, whether from physical deficiencies or legal restrictions.

Mark's composition emphasizes the antithetical relationship that exists between Jesus' release of God's life-giving power and the response of the religious leaders to it. While Jesus is restoring life through God's power, his opponents plot to take his life from him. Mark's emphasis shows clearly that doing harm and taking life contradict Jesus' own actions and are, therefore, inauthentic responses to God's life-restoring initiative.

The religious leaders justify Jesus' death sentence by their Sabbath tradition. They had decided that the Sabbath was a law to be obeyed regardless of human cost. Consequently, they would use the law to halt even God's initiatives. Mark notes that their hearts are so hardened that they only care that a law must be broken if suffering would be alleviated. Their compassion has been subordinated to rigid adherence to rules and laws. So, not only do they plot to take Jesus' life from him because he "worked" on the Sabbath, they would also choose to do nothing to ease a man's suffering because it is the Sabbath. Denise Lardner Carmody insists that religion is at its "most ugly" when it behaves in this manner.[15] Unfortunately, such religion neither began nor ended with Jesus' opponents. Who among us has not encountered a church where rules mattered more than compassion? Jesus' anger clearly denotes that hardened, compassionless hearts, rigid adherence to law, and choosing to do nothing in the face of suffering are inauthentic responses to the compassionate God of Life who is moved by human need.

Jesus expects his followers to be active and choose to do good and save life as he did. His actions reveal these responses to be authentic ones to God's initiatives to benefit people and release life-resurrecting power. Furthermore, he expects the Sabbath to be viewed as a perfect day for doing good and saving life. Here is another authentic response to God's gift in this story. The occurrence of this healing on the Sabbath points to Jesus as Lord of the Sabbath who is inaugurating the *basileia* of God that the Sabbath symbolized and who proclaims that God's laws are meant to serve God's people. If a religion that has subordinated compassion to law is most ugly, one that shows compassion to those who suffer is most beautiful,[16] for this is God's own attitude.

Finally, after studying two texts that show Jesus in conflict with the religious leaders (over purity laws, 7:1–23; over Sabbath laws, 3:1–6), we can clearly see how Mark believed he was turning their view of spirituality upside down. Mark's Jesus was not refining their understanding of relationship with God, he was subverting it. Their focus was law; his was people. No wonder Mark records Jesus saying, "No one puts new wine into old wineskins . . . but new wine is for new skins" (2:22). No wonder Jesus called his hearers to repent, to reorient their lives according to the vision of the Gospel (1:15).[17]

We can see just as clearly that the religious leaders were not open to this new wine from God. Such a lack of openness to newness is an inauthentic response to the God of Jesus who surprises in so many ways. Reorienting our lives, opening ourselves to God's new revelations, new commands, new ways of being, and the like are authentic responses to Mark's God of surprise. Furthermore, we can speculate as to why the religious leaders were so invested in the old wine. They had honor (as interpreters of the law) and privilege over others (places in the court nearer the Holy of Holies in the Temple; also note 12:38–39) in the old order which they might not wish to lose.[18] If such speculation is accurate, then we can describe more clearly the difference between Jesus and the religious leaders: Their focus was law and themselves as interpreters of law; Jesus' focus was others and their needs. The religious leaders' focus caused them to be closed to both

God's new initiatives and others' needs. Clearly their concerns for law, honor, and personal privilege are inauthentic responses to God. Perhaps religious leaders today should ask themselves whom they imitate most often—Jesus or Jesus' opponents.

Mark 4:35–41

In the middle of Jesus' ministry in Galilee, Mark presents a group of miracles that show off Jesus' power. The first of these miracles, the stilling of the storm (4:35–41), immediately follows the parables discourse (4:1–34). Indeed, the temporal notation "on that day" (4:35) is probably intended to link this miracle of Jesus with his just completed parabolic teaching. Consequently, this nature miracle serves as a manifestation to the disciples of the mystery of the *basileia* of God that Jesus had just revealed to them in the parables.

The stilling of the storm and the three miracles that follow (the Gerasene demoniac, 5:1–20; Jairus's daughter, 5:21–24, 35–43; the hemorrhaging woman, 5:25–34) are extraordinary, even more so than miracles usually are. Each is described as a response to a situation that appeared hopeless. Someone turned to Jesus when all human efforts had been exhausted. Furthermore, in each there is a contrast between the spontaneous response of the witnesses and the one Jesus preferred them to have.[19] Thus any of these stories offers a fine opportunity for studying God's initiatives and the responses to them. The first story is chosen because of its relation to the parables discourse and its uniqueness as a nature miracle in this collection of miracles.

While this series of extraordinary miracles may have come to Mark from the oral traditions of the early church, he had a definitive hand in their final shape in his Gospel. We note Mark's editorial work especially in the prominence accorded the motif of fear. Though a reaction of wonder, awe, or fear may be typical of miracle stories, this fact cannot explain the prevalence Mark grants to it, especially in the dual references to the disciples' fear in verses 40–41.[20] Significantly, these notices about the disciples' fear occur after Jesus stilled the storm. By contrast, in Matthew, Jesus stills the storm because the disciples are afraid (Matt. 8:23–27). In Mark, however, the disciples' fear is more than an emotional reaction to the storm so that its abatement intensifies rather than ends their fearfulness. In addition, fear is specifically contrasted with faith in verse 40. Therefore, the search for authentic and inauthentic responses to God's initiatives in this story must pay attention to the response of fear in it and to the faith against which the fear is juxtaposed.

God's Initiatives

The miracle Jesus performs in this story is the stilling of a destructive storm that had risen against him and his disciples (perhaps still the larger group of 4:10) as they crossed the Sea of Galilee. Mark paints two particular nuances on the power of God in the telling of this story. First, he has cast this nature miracle as an exorcism story. Jesus, having been roused from sleep by frantic disciples, rebuked the wind and told the sea to be silent. These verbs throughout Mark, especially "rebuked," are commands by which the demonic forces opposed to God are overcome (note 1:25).[21] Their use here suggests Mark's view that a personal source of trouble is at work in the storm on the sea which Jesus must overcome.[22]

The sea had become, by Mark's day, symbolic of the powers of evil and chaos. As such a symbol, it reflects the ancient Near Easterners' (Jews included) identification of the sea with the forces of evil. This identification was derived from the stories in various cultures of the original act of creation that involved God in a desperate but finally victorious contest with the forces of evil which were located in the sea. By conquering the sea, God created the orderly world out of the primeval chaos. The sea continued among the Jews as a metaphor for the evil forces active in the world and particularly for the trials of the righteous from which only God could deliver them (see Pss. 18:16; 69:1–2, 14–15).[23] Mark has followed suit and cast the sea as a source of evil that Jesus rebukes and subdues.

The second nuance cast on God's initiative may also be found in the terminology that stills the sea. It has been borrowed from stories of Yahweh's stilling of the hostile sea (e.g., Job 26:10–12) and used by Jesus here as he re-creates the harmony of the universe by reclaiming it from Satan's dominion.[24] By so acting, Mark's Jesus has done what, in the Hebrew Bible, only God can do. The power both to still the raging sea (see Job 26:12; Isa. 51:15; Jer. 31:35; Pss. 89:9–10; 107:29) and to trample on the back of the sea (Job 9:8; Hab. 3:15; Ps. 77:19) belong to God alone. Thus Mark's picture of Jesus calming the sea shows him exercising divine control over nature. Therefore the story is epiphanic—it reveals the divine presence in Jesus.[25]

Mark heightens the sense of the divine presence even more by picturing Jesus asleep in the boat as the storm begins (4:38). In the ancient Near East the motif of the sleeping deity functioned as a statement of the deity's absolute dominion over the universe; because of this dominion the deity could afford to sleep. The motif is employed frequently in the Hebrew Bible (see Isa. 51:9–11). The image of the sleeping Jesus in this story may be modeled after this motif. If so, his sleep indicates neither fatigue nor powerlessness but rather his possession of absolute authority, indeed the very power of God. The power of evil is only apparent as seen when Jesus stills the raging sea.[26]

Thus the story's nuances emphasize that God's initiatives here are being present with the disciples in Jesus and unleashing divine power through Jesus to silence the forces of evil that threaten the disciples' lives. If indeed this story is a manifestation of the mystery of the *basileia* of God that was just revealed to the disciples in the parables (4:1–34), then the mystery may be further understood as the presence and power of God at work in the peasant carpenter Jesus to overcome the demonic powers and replace them with the peace of the *basileia* of God.

The Responses

Following the arrival of the calm after the storm, Jesus chided his disciples, "Why are you afraid? Do you still not have faith?" (4:40). Neither faith nor fear has been explicitly mentioned in this story until its end. Here they receive emphasis. Thus Jesus' question forms the climax of the story and reveals a distinctive purpose in Mark's version of the story.[27] Mark was specifically interested in these responses of disciples to the presence of divine power in Jesus that stilled the storm.

The fear of the disciples is often understood as cowardice, a common human fear of losing one's life due to the intensity of the storm. Then, using this understanding of the fear, scholars explain that the disciples lack faith in Jesus' power to save their lives from the storm.[28] When the disciples awakened Jesus, however, they asked him, "Teacher, is it of no concern to you that we perish?" (v. 38). Their question was more, "Do you not care enough to do anything?" than, "Can you not do anything?" It may even be read as a sarcastic jab at Jesus for sleeping while they do all the work to keep the boat afloat. They make no request of him; they apparently expect nothing out of the ordinary from him. Comparison with Matthew and Luke is instructive. Both of them (Matt. 8:25, "Lord, save us! We are perishing!"; Luke 8:24, "Master! Master! We are perishing!") soften the words of the disciples by removing the implied charge—sarcastic or otherwise—that Jesus does not care enough to act. Both of them indicate the fearfulness of the disciples and their desperate plea that Jesus save them from that which they cannot save themselves. Mark has none of this in his version of the story.

Not until after Jesus stilled the storm does Mark signal that the disciples felt any fear. When the calm came (v. 39b), Jesus then asked them, "Why are you afraid?" (v. 40a) and, "Do you still not have faith?" (v. 40b). Mark follows Jesus' words by telling readers that the disciples "feared a great fear" (literal translation of v. 41a). The best clue for understanding the disciples' fear is found in the question they then ask one another, "Who is this that even the wind and sea obey him?" (v. 41b). Their question is rhetorical. Since only God can command the wind and sea, they see exactly who Jesus is. It is precisely this knowledge that terrifies them.

The disciples' fear, therefore, is the sense of numinous awe toward the "wholly other" or *mysterium tremendum,*[29] which is described in many texts in the Hebrew Bible and New Testament as the fear of God's presence, of God coming and acting in the realm in which we actually live.[30] John Donahue has noted that Mark stresses the mystery and transcendence of God throughout his Gospel.[31] We should say, more accurately for this story, that Mark stresses the "awe-full" mystery and transcendence of God brought near to ordinary human beings in Jesus. Thus the NRSV translation of verse 41a, "They were filled with great awe," is exact. The problem for the disciples is not that they do not know who Jesus is; their problem after the stilling of the storm is that they know exactly who he is.

Is their awe an authentic or inauthentic response to God? The story is ambiguous since it ends on the note about the disciples' awe with neither Jesus nor Mark commenting on it. Clarification can be found in the other stupendous miracles of this collection (5:1–43). Numinous awe is a significant part of each of these stories.

Following the healing of the Gerasene demoniac (5:1–12), the people came to see what had happened. When they saw the demoniac, whom no one had been able to subdue even with chains, sitting with Jesus, clothed and in his right mind, they were afraid (5:15). This fear, which is the result of such an incredible miracle, must also be that sense of awe before the power of God. But the people responded by begging Jesus to leave their region (5:17). They apparently did not want God coming and acting in the realm in which they live. Did they sense that too much would be demanded of them, that God's presence might call for repentance, for their worlds to be subverted? Whatever, they allowed their awe to become literal fear. They were closed to Jesus and pushed him away. The healed demoniac, in contrast, begged Jesus to be allowed to be with him (5:18). Since Mark noted earlier that Jesus called disciples so that they might be with him (3:14), the demoniac's response must be an acceptable one, though Jesus had other work for the demoniac to do (5:19). Rudolf Otto noted that numinous awe has an aspect of both dread and attraction.[32] This story suggests that Jesus expects disciples to be attracted to the power and presence of God as the demoniac was, to trust that the presence of God and the reorientation it demands is for their good, rather than to dread it, fear it, and turn from it as the townspeople did.

On the way to the home of Jairus, the woman with a hemorrhage touched Jesus' garment and was healed (5:29). When Jesus asked who had touched him, the woman, "fearing and trembling because she knew what had happened to her," came forward (5:33). The contrast with Luke helps to clarify her fear. In Luke's story the woman trembled and fell before Jesus when she realized she was not hidden (Luke 8:47). Mark's woman, however, knew what had happened to her body and as a result of that knowledge feared and trembled. Therefore, her fear appears again to be a sense of numinous awe.[33] She did not, however, allow her sense of awe to become literal fear and drive her from Jesus. Instead she came and fell before him and told him the whole truth (5:33). That her response was appropriate is seen in Jesus' reaction to her: "Your faith has saved you. Go in peace" (5:34).

As this episode ended, word reached Jairus that his daughter had died (5:35). Jesus told Jairus, "Do not fear; only have faith" (5:36). The words "do not fear" are surprising here since the death is not threatening but has already happened. Words such as "do not grieve" would seem to have been more appropriate.[34] Such being the case, and since this story frames that of the woman with a hemorrhage, Jesus' charge to Jairus may be a call to trust the power of God—power that is awe-full enough to raise the dead—to do good for him and not to dread it, fear it, or turn from it. Jairus apparently did not dread Jesus' power, for he allowed Jesus into his house. He received his daughter back as a result (5:42).

This review of the other miracles in Mark's collection suggests that numinous awe is a normal human response to the nearness of the divine presence and is, by itself, neutral. The key question is how a person responds to such an experience of awe. The inauthentic response is to be overcome with a sense of dread of what the near presence of God might demand, to allow the awe to become "just plain fear," and, therefore, to desire distance from the *mysterium tremendum* that aroused the awe. The townspeople who came out to see the Gerasene demoniac are examples of those who respond so inauthentically.

The authentic response is, first, to be attracted, to be drawn to the divine presence and power as was the woman with the hemorrhage. Authentic disciples are able to draw near to the wholly other because they have faith that the power and presence of God and whatever reorientation it might demand are for their good. Persons making this response have faith that the divine power unleashed by Jesus is packaged in love and directed toward human beings in need. This faith is the second authentic response to the power and presence of God revealed in the story of Jesus stilling the storm.

Summary of Mark 4:35–41

God's initiatives here may be understood from two aspects of this story. First, God's initiative is seen in the emphasis placed on God being present in Jesus with disciples. Second, God's initiative is noted in the divine power unleashed through Jesus against the evil that threatened the lives of disciples. By the power of God, Jesus overcame the demonic element epitomized in the chaos of the storm on the sea because that element is at enmity with God and, therefore, with God's creature, humanity.

The competing responses to these initiatives may be clearly discerned in Mark's having emphasized Jesus' questions to his disciples, "Why are you afraid? Do you still not have faith?" (4:40). When Mark then noted that the disciples "feared a great fear" (v. 41a), he indicated they were filled with that sense of numinous awe that human beings experience when they realize they are in the presence of the divine, the wholly other. It is possible, in response to this sense of awe, for disciples to be filled with dread before the divine presence, literally to fear it, and turn away from God. They may sense God's presence would demand that they change, call for repentance, and subvert their worlds, and not be open to such. The contrast between the behavior of the townspeople and the demoniac in the Gerasene story demonstrates the inauthenticity of this response of fear, dread, and turning away. Jesus' questions to his disciples likewise call them away from this fear.

What does Jesus expect from them instead? The sense of awe felt by the woman with the hemorrhage when she knew she had been healed did not stop her from coming to Jesus when he called her forward. His words to her, "Daughter, your faith has saved you. Go in peace" (5:34), demonstrate the authenticity of her response. Jesus expects disciples to be attracted to the *mysterium tremendum* that is the source of the awe. He expects disciples to have faith that God's presence and power, along with whatever repentance is called forth, are for their good. He expects his followers to believe that God's power comes packaged in love and is unleashed on behalf of human beings in need. Attraction to and faith in God's presence and power in Jesus are authentic responses to God's initiatives.

Mark 7:24–30

Following his confrontation with the religious leaders over purity in 7:1–23 (discussed in chapter 2), Jesus embarks on his first extended travels into Gentile country where he is immediately encountered by a Syrophoenician woman (7:24–30). I have selected the story of this meeting because it is one of several exorcism stories for which Mark is known, it is one of several stories in Mark involving Jesus and women, it is unique in Mark as a miracle involving distance, and finally, because its concern for the inclusion of Gentiles in God's salvation means it takes up the purity issue raised in Mark 7:1–23.

Some oddities about this story, however, create problems for this study. The encounter is cast as a miracle story, but the dialogue between Jesus and the woman dominates the action. Furthermore, the woman bests Jesus in their verbal exchange—the only person in Mark's story to do so. At first Jesus refuses to grant the woman's request but then is talked into it. Indeed, Jesus is not the protagonist in this story—the woman is. Her actions and words push the incident to its conclusion. Jesus, by contrast, initiates nothing.[35]

These oddities, especially the scant attention given the miracle and Jesus' lack of initiative, might suggest that this story is not a good one for this study. I have chosen instead to view the oddities as potentially revelatory of an aspect of Markan spirituality that might otherwise be missed. They will require, however, an "odd" treatment of this text compared to others in this study. I have found it most helpful to review the whole story in detail in order to discern God's initiatives.

God's Initiatives

After the story of the purity confrontation, Mark's narrative brings Jesus into the Gentile territory of Tyre, north of Galilee (7:24a). The geography is more than accidental. Jesus' rebuke of the religious leaders over clean hands and food in 7:1–23 is intensified by his movements as he leaves the land and people who are "clean" to enter a land that is "unclean."[36] In the Hebrew Bible, Tyre is said to be proud and a threat to the Israelites and is always recorded with Sidon as polluted by materialism (e.g., Isa. 23, Ezek. 27—28). Jesus' crossing the border into this land, therefore, is symbolic of his subversion of the religious leaders' view of purity.[37]

In Tyre, Jesus is immediately approached, despite his efforts to hide, by a woman whose daughter has an "unclean spirit" (7:25). Mark identifies the woman as a Greek and a Syrophoenician by birth (v. 26). Women from Tyre or the area of Phoenicia were connected to ancient Jewish struggles with foreign religious practices, particularly that of temple prostitution. Consequently, the term "Syrophoenician" was sometimes used to denote a woman from the seamier side of the city.[38] The text thus suggests she is not only a Gentile but also a pagan whose sexual behavior is suspect. Suspicion about her status is heightened by her apparent isolation from family support. If there had been a male relative, he would have had the responsibility for caring for her and her daughter.[39] The lack of a male relative could have pushed her into prostitution for survival.

She came and fell down at Jesus' feet (7:25). No Jewish man, especially one with a religious vocation, expected to be approached by a woman, especially one unknown and unrelated to Jews.[40] But to have her bow down at his feet! Such behavior was acceptable among men, but for a woman to do so does not honor Jesus as a teacher. On the contrary, it disgraces him.[41] She so acts on behalf of her daughter, which is a further liability. Sons were the focus of one's hopes and one's longing. Daughters were often regarded as troublesome pieces of property weighing on their families until suitable husbands could be found (then they cost a dowry!).[42] Finally, readers are told this daughter was possessed by "an unclean spirit"—Mark's usual designation is "demon" as in 7:26, 29, 30. The issue of demon-possession requires consideration (especially for twentieth-century Western readers), but since the exorcism itself is so peripheral to this story, that discussion will be held until study of Mark 9:14–29. Here the detail of the unclean spirit completes the portrait of a thoroughly unclean woman, according to that culture: foreign, female, pagan, seamy, inappropriately assertive, possessed by an unclean spirit.

Therefore, Jesus' response to her, "Let the children be fed first, for it is not good to take the children's bread and throw it to the little dogs" (7:27), would have been entirely fitting in that culture.[43] Readers of Mark's Gospel, however, usually find his words troubling. While some scholars try to show that Jesus meant a cozy household scene where even the children's little puppies were fed from the abundance of the messianic banquet, the stark reality against the backdrop of first-century Mediterranean culture is that "little dog" was a term of reproach for a woman, especially a Gentile woman, who had behaved shamelessly. Jesus compared the woman and her people to dogs and refused her request because she was not of his people.[44] Oddly enough, Jesus had already healed a foreigner—the Gerasene demoniac from whom he had exorcised an unclean spirit (5:1–13). Perhaps his refusal here is due to the woman's "extreme" impurity.

Considering Jesus' subversion of the external view of purity in the immediately preceding story, however (and how unaccustomed we are to Jesus using insulting language), Mark's readers are often disturbed by Jesus' response. If the story of the stilling of the storm highlighted the divine presence with Jesus, this story appears to emphasize the human Jesus. Though he had taught others that externals, boundaries, and surfaces had nothing to do with a person's purity, it appears that now he also must learn the radical dimensions of his own proclamation.

This "unclean" woman will be his teacher. She would not accept the low esteem in which her culture held her daughter or its restrictions on her own behavior.[45] Despite Jesus' harsh refusal, she risks moving from insult to humiliation by persisting in her request: "But she answered and said to him, 'Yes, Lord, even the dogs under the table are eating from the children's crumbs'" (7:28). She takes his term of reproach and turns it around. She is the one who evokes a household scene, speaking of dogs as though she meant pets which became cherished parts of a family.[46] The woman contends that even if Jesus' words are true, acts of dignity and charity are not excluded. If dogs eat crumbs under the table, how can Jesus deny her? Is he not gracious enough to provide at least crumbs?[47]

In addition, she addresses him as "Lord," the only person in Mark's story to do so. In contrast to all the "clean" onlookers, this woman "sees" who Jesus is and holds him to it, refusing to settle for a diminishment of the promise of God. Suppressing any feelings of fear and hesitation she might have, this woman persists, knowing she and her daughter must gain life, and Jesus can grant it to them.[48] A number of scholars have claimed that she freed Jesus to be who he truly was. Her desperate argument enabled him to become again the channel of God's redeeming presence,[49] which he did when he granted her request. He told her, "Because of this word [i.e., her argument], go. The demon has left your daughter" (7:29). By finally healing her daughter as she asked, Jesus accepted her as worthy of his time and attention and of God's healing power.[50] Hisako Kinukawa described the climactic moment well:

> Jesus, "the boundary-breaker," may not have needed the encounter with her to cross the racial barrier, but certainly it is the woman that has created the opportunity for him to cross it and step over to her side. . . . Her intuition about who Jesus should be and Jesus' sensitivity to the marginalized are drawn into one vortex and create a mutual transformation.[51]

Not incidentally, the woman took Jesus at his word even about a healing at a distance, went home, and found her daughter well (7:30). Her actions indicate great faith.

Now that we have seen the story to its conclusion, we are in position to see God's initiatives at work. First, the story clearly demonstrates that God places no "external" barriers (external purity requirements) between God and humanity and indeed is working to remove any such barriers that people might erect. Jesus had already said as much in the purity discourse in 7:1–23. He acts out this reality in this story. The oddities in the narrative—the woman's extreme "impurity," Jesus' initial troubling response, her persistence, and his final acquiescence—serve to emphasize that race, class, ethnicity, and gender play no role in God's acceptance of a person no matter how convinced human beings are that they do. Furthermore, the list of external "nonbarriers" is lengthened in Mark's Gospel when Jesus touches a leper (1:40–44) and welcomes children (10:13–16): neither physical condition (disease) nor age limits access to God's *basileia*.

Second, Jesus' ultimate endorsement of this desperate, persistent woman reveals God's openness to and acceptance of the wrestling, questioning, demanding, hurting side of humanity. The God portrayed here does not require polite, passive piety that pretends everything is fine when pain abounds. Instead, this God is the one with whom Jesus pleads in Gethsemane (14:36), and the one at whom he screams from the cross (15:34). God's continuing acceptance of Jesus after these audacious words is made clear when God vindicates him by raising him from the dead (16:6). Likewise, God's acceptance of this demanding, desperate woman is demonstrated by the healing of her daughter.

The Responses

The authentic responses that are called forth by these initiatives of God begin with faith that is no mere doctrinal confession but an act of trust, of engagement.[52] This faith requires "sight" as in Mark 4:21–25, courage, and bold, assertive action on behalf of someone loved. The Syrophoenician woman "saw" Jesus as Lord and thus risked utter humiliation (in a culture that valued honor above all else) to speak up for and then argue on behalf of her sick daughter. Gail O'Day has written that this woman stands fully in the tradition of Abraham, Moses, and those who prayed the psalms of lament who were not afraid to argue with God, who refused to let go of the promises of God.[53] A faith like this woman's gambles everything on the faithfulness of God.

A second authentic response depends on the first. God's initiative in this story also calls forth recognition that there are no external barriers between God and any human being: not race, class, ethnicity, gender, age, or physical condition. Consequently, there should also be no such barriers between human beings. If no one is "not good enough" for God, then there can be no one who is "not good enough" for other human beings. Apparently such openness to all others is difficult for human beings to accept, even Jesus struggled to do so! Whether Jew or Gentile, male or female, ancient or modern, we all encounter so much in our cultures that is intent on devaluing those who are different. Therefore, insightful, courageous faith is indeed necessary to see others as God sees them and to live with others as God intends so that authentic disciples counter any culture's oppressive, discriminatory attitudes and actions toward others.

The inauthentic responses Mark calls readers to turn from are discovered by considering what would be opposite the authentic responses. This story adds emphasis to the teaching of 7:1–23 that practicing an external purity is an inauthentic response to God who erects no external barriers between God and humanity and removes the ones people create. However difficult it may be to remain uninfluenced by society's negative evaluations of persons who are somehow different, to be prejudiced thusly is to respond inauthentically to God who judges persons' hearts.

Furthermore, the story teaches that an inability or unwillingness to hold to God's promises, indeed a lack of trust in God's faithfulness that leads to making safe, timid choices that protect ourselves when others need us to be bold on their behalf is an inauthentic response to God who accepts the wrestling, demanding side of humanity. Hiding behind a polite, passive piety when courageous, assertive action (which might put us at risk) could bring someone to wholeness is not the response Mark believed that God desired.

Summary of Mark 7:24–30

Through review of the unusual aspects of this story, we discovered that God has taken the initiative through Jesus to actualize the teaching of the purity discourse (7:1–23). God places no external boundaries (race, class, ethnicity, gender, age, physical condition) between God and any human being. Indeed, God through Jesus is shattering any such barriers people may try to erect.

Further, God accepts the wrestling, questioning, demanding, hurting side of humanity that leads persons to plead, argue, even scream at God. God does not demand a polite, passive piety. Instead, Jesus' healing of the woman's daughter because of her argument demonstrates that God is open to bold, assertive, faithful action on behalf of loved ones.

Therefore, a timid faith that makes safe choices for oneself is not acceptable, is an inauthentic response to God. A primary example of a timid, inauthentic choice, according to this story, is an unwillingness to challenge and cross over the external barriers people create between God and others and also between themselves and others. This unwillingness is also an inauthentic response to God. Instead, Mark understands God to call for a bold, assertive, insightful faith that refuses to relinquish God's promises. One thing a person acting on such faith "sees" is the absence of any external barriers between God and people. Therefore, authentically faithful disciples confront and cross over any such barriers people construct. This story also warns that courageous faith is necessary for these confrontations, for people will resist having their external purity boundaries demolished. Even Jesus struggled to accept the implications of God's radical inclusion of all humanity in God's *basileia*.

Chapter 4

Responding to God
Who Ransoms and Reveals
Suffering and
Vindication

We return now to the task begun in
chapter 2: to uncover God's initiatives and the authentic and inauthentic responses to them in Jesus' parabolic words. In this chapter we
focus on the second half of Mark's Gospel, examining Jesus' teachings
on the way to Jerusalem (8:31–9:1; 9:30–37; 10:32–45) and his last
long discourse, which occurs in Jerusalem itself (13:1–37).

Mark 8:31–9:1; 9:30–37; 10:32–45

A major part of what Mark's Jesus taught occurs, though not in
continuous discourse, throughout the narrative of Jesus' journey to
Jerusalem (8:27–10:52) during which he tries to prepare disciples for
his passion. The religious authorities, so much in evidence before and
after this section, appear during the journey only twice in marginal
roles. The disciples are clearly the focus of attention instead.

This section of Mark is a well-constructed segment presented as a
journey from the villages of Caesarea Philippi to Jerusalem. The sense
of movement is highlighted by the recurring phrase "on the way."
"The way" that Jesus goes is not only a literal journey to Jerusalem,
however. It is also intended to be understood spiritually.[1] The "way
of the Lord" in this part of Mark involves following Jesus "on the way"
to Jerusalem and the cross.

The section is organized around three predictions of Jesus' sufferings. The movement in the predictions is a crescendo, so that the last
one is the most explicit and detailed. Each of the predictions is followed by disciples' misunderstanding which in turn prompts Jesus'
attempts to correct them. The manner in which the prediction-
misunderstanding-correction pattern has been edited suggests Mark's

creative work.[2] The threefold repetition of the pattern indicates that Mark was underscoring something he considered important for would-be followers of Jesus.

The pattern presents a convenient means of studying this section of Mark for the spirituality contained therein. Jesus' predictions offer God's initiatives to reveal the significance of the mission and destiny of both Jesus and his followers. The misunderstandings of disciples present obvious examples of inauthentic responses to God's initiatives. The corrective teachings contain the authentic responses sought by Jesus to God's initiatives.

The Passion Predictions: God's Initiatives

Mark's Jesus reveals to his disciples in the passion predictions that he must suffer and die before being raised after three days (8:31; 9:31; 10:33–34). But it is not just the fact of Jesus' suffering that is emphasized. The use of the word "must" in 8:31—the Son of man/New Human Being[3] *must* die—indicates that Jesus' passion accomplishes the will of God. The Greek word for "must" is used here as it often is in apocalyptic literature to indicate that certain future events are part of the divine purpose.[4] Thus Jesus' suffering and death are viewed as divinely conditioned necessities. These things must occur. They are not catastrophes. They are part of the fulfillment of the divine plan. God has taken the initiative to reveal their necessity through Jesus to disciples.

How are we to understand Jesus' suffering as God's will? Is God a sadist who demands the sacrifice of Jesus to appease God's sense of justice?[5] Christians throughout the centuries would answer that question with a resounding no! They would say they have not experienced God as such, though preachers and theologians have sometimes made God sound like such. How then is Jesus' suffering part of the divine plan? Ched Myers has suggested that the "must" in Mark should be understood as "inevitable"; it is inevitable that Jesus die.[6] We have seen that Jesus' inauguration of the *basileia* of God through his teachings and miracles subverts the world to which his hearers are accustomed. Those who benefit from the world as is—the religious and political elites—are not interested in changing the circumstances that serve them well. Because they sit atop the current world, they have power at their disposal to oppose those seeking change. History shows us they will usually use it (e.g., consider the response to the efforts to end apartheid in South Africa). Despite their opposition, however, Jesus continues to pursue God's *basileia* in accordance with God's will. Thus his suffering at their hands is inevitable.

Mark's Jesus illustrates through allegory this response to God's will by those in power in his parable of the vineyard owner (12:1–12). The allusion to Isaiah 5:1–7 in Mark 12:1 indicates that God is the vineyard owner who plants a vineyard, which represents Israel or, more broadly, the people of God. God's great concern for God's people is portrayed in the care and attention the vineyard owner gives to the vineyard: setting a hedge around it, digging a pit for the winepress, building a tower, and putting tenants over it to cultivate it (12:1). But these tenants decide they want the vineyard for themselves (v. 7) and resort to violence to get it (vv. 3–5). Indeed, when the vineyard owner, against all common sense and beyond all reasonable expectations of repentance and rightness, sends the "beloved son" (v. 6), the tenants see a chance to close the deal. Significantly, it is because they recognize the beloved son that they kill him (vv. 7–8). They want for themselves what is rightfully his—the vineyard and the right to "tend" the people of God.[7] They are clearly interested only in their gain. The owner who cared for the vineyard is not their concern. Therefore, the suffering of God's servants and even of God's son at their hands is inevitable.

The tenants in the parable represent the religious leaders of Jesus' day, an identification even they recognize (12:12). Several recent scholars have noted the injustices of absentee landownership in first-century Palestine and that the religious leaders were often absentee landowners themselves.[8] Ched Myers suggests that those hearing this parable might "revel in the role-reversal that demoted the ruling class to the lowly status of unruly tenants."[9] But there is also a more generalized application: The tenants would represent any group in power that obstructs the fruitfulness (remember the parable of the sower) of God's people.[10]

Twentieth-century Christians have witnessed a number of events that illustrate the inevitability of suffering for those who would subvert the world in favor of the *basileia* of God. Reflection on the stories of those who have been martyred by contemporary evil "tenants" such as Dietrich Bonhoeffer, Martin Luther King Jr., and other civil rights activists, or Archbishop Romero and the four murdered nuns in

El Salvador (among others) further enables us to "see" the inevitability of Jesus' death.

Two key observations sharpen our understanding and prevent misunderstanding of Jesus' suffering in Mark. First, Mark's Jesus does not attach any suffering (cancer, floods, war, etc.) to the accomplishment of the will of God but only suffering that is the result of proclaiming the *basileia* of God. Consider how precisely Mark makes this point in 4:17 ("when trouble or persecution arises *on account of the word*") and 8:35 ("those who lose their lives *for my sake and the gospel*") (emphasis mine). Second, the religious and political elites are responsible for Jesus' suffering in Mark, not "the Jews."[11] Anti-Semitic Christians who have justified their hatred by calling Jews Christ killers have conveniently ignored both the Jewishness of Jesus' first followers and the specific identity of his opponents. Jesus' enemies in Mark were not the Jews but the religous elites (Pharisees, priests, scribes) and political powers (Herodians, Romans) who conspired to destroy Jesus before he destroyed their status, privilege, and honor. Note that in the parable of the vineyard owner it is the tenants (the religious leaders), not the vineyard (Israel), that the vineyard owner judges (12:9).[12] When we specify Jesus' enemies, we can see how the suffering of Jesus was inevitable.

In these verses, then, God has taken the initiative to reveal to followers of Jesus the cost of proclaiming God's *basileia*. We might add that by doing so God has also shown that God is brutally honest with God's people.

Mark also believed that Jesus found in his own suffering and death profound spiritual meaning. Mark 10:45 discloses that meaning: Jesus announced that he gave his life as "a ransom for many." Among the possible interpretations for "ransom" is its use to indicate a price paid to free slaves. Such an interpretation of it in v. 45 would indicate that Jesus' action is for the benefit of others, for freeing them from the things that enslave them.[13]

Scholars and preachers have often understood this ransom to be from sin.[14] I suggest, however, that such an interpretation of ranson is based more on traditional Christian doctrine than on a careful reading of Mark's Gospel. In fact, Mark records Jesus' mentioning sin in only four instances: he forgave the sin of the paralyzed man who was let down through the roof (2:1–12), declared that he had come to call sinners (2:17), warned that all sins can be forgiven except that of blaspheming the Holy Spirit (3:28–30), and told followers they must forgive others if they would have God forgive their sins (11:25). Two points clarify our understanding of sin in relation to ransom in Mark. First, Jesus forgave sin (in the story of the paralyzed man) before his death, and, thus, before it could be a ransom for sin. Second, "sinners" in Mark's world were marginal people who were badly paid, often abused, ostracized from the community (for working at a disreputable job like tax collecting or fishing or selling fruit, for not keeping the purity rules, or for not paying taxes, etc.), and in need of restoration, not those who do bad things and then are ravaged by the resulting guilt as twentieth-century Western Christians often think[15].

Certainly Mark knew about wrong actions, attitudes, and choices people make (note 7:21–22) that today we usually name "sin." But Mark does not appear to view sin as that which keeps people in bondage from which they need to be ransomed (as Paul does, e.g., in Rom. 5:12–21). Instead in Mark's Gospel thus far we have seen people enslaved by demonic powers, purity rules based on surfaces and boundaries, rigid legalism, attachment to honor and status, fear of persecution, even fear of God drawing near. Later we will add to this list when we see how oppressive the Temple economic system was. By calling his death a ransom for many, Mark's Jesus specified it as the initiative of God to remove these forms of bondage so that people are free to live as God intended in God's *basileia*. Thus Mark interprets Jesus' death as God's initiative to provide an "exodus from slavery" rather than a "sacrifice of atonement."[16] He does not say how Jesus' death liberates people from oppression. By naming it a ransom, however, he clearly declares that it does so liberate.

The Misunderstandings: Inauthentic Responses

Mark interprets Peter's response to Jesus' first announcement of his suffering with two verbs that express superiority (8:32): "Having taken Jesus [the Greek word for "having taken" conveys the idea of coming alongside and taking over as one does with children or the sick[17]], Peter began to rebuke him [the Greek word translated as "rebuke" is the same word used by Jesus to rebuke demons during exorcisms in 1:25; 9:25]." Thus Mark shows Peter not only missing the significance of Jesus' suffering, but to the extent that Peter does understand what Jesus said he rejects—even rebukes—the notion.[18] He does not see Jesus' passion as accomplishing God's will, that God would not prevent the suffering of God's own people for the sake of the *basileia*. Like the partially healed man who saw people as trees walking (8:23–24), Peter sees Jesus indistinctly—he can see the Christ (8:29) but not the suffering Son of man/New Human Being (8:31). In his blindness he reacts with the "instinct" of human beings whose first thought is to save themselves.[19] The inauthenticity of Peter's response to Jesus' revelation is underscored by Jesus' rebuking him and declaring that Peter was "thinking of human things" rather than the things of God (8:33). Here again in sharp relief is the conflict between the Way of the Lord and the Way of Humanity.

The inauthentic responses to God in this passage are quite clear: not accepting that suffering for God's *basileia* accomplishes God's purposes, and seeking to save oneself in the face of such potential suffering.

Following Jesus' second prediction of his suffering, Mark relates that the disciples did not understand and were afraid to ask (9:32). We have already seen that lack of understanding is an inauthentic response to God's revealing activity (4:11–13). But the disciples are not through responding inauthentically. In the discussion that follows they argued among themselves who was the greatest (9:33–34); that is, they were squabbling over honor status in the group, seeking to sit atop the pecking order there. Indeed they did not understand that Jesus sought the subversion of their world, that his new wine did not fit into old wineskins. They did not grasp that any pecking order was inherently oppressive because it puts a few on top while the rest reside beneath them, under their control, and thus not free. It appears that the disciples wanted to play the same game but with a different set of players (themselves) in the privileged positions. Jesus, however, was introducing a completely different game as he came to ransom people from whatever oppressed them. Furthermore, Mark has heightened the irony of the disciples' concern for their own honor in the face of Jesus' acceptance of the inevitability of his suffering by emphasizing that the discussion about who was the greatest occurred "on the way" (i.e., on the way to Jerusalem and the cross, 9:33–34). The contrast between Jesus' reception of his suffering to free others for God's *basileia* and the disciples' desire for honor and privilege for themselves shows the inauthenticity of their response.

The final passion prediction is preceded by a specific note that the group was on its way to Jerusalem, Jesus was going before them, and the disciples were amazed and afraid (10:32). These strong emotions imply that the disciples saw what could lie at the end of their journey.

But incredibly, following Jesus' last and most detailed prediction of his coming travail (10:33–34), James and John approach Jesus and ask to sit at his right and left hands when he comes in his glory (10:37). Instead of being concerned for Jesus' plight or what he was trying to teach them, James and John continued to seek positions of honor, status, and privilege over Jesus' followers. The other ten were indignant at their request (10:41), thus manifesting the same concern for honor as James and John.[20] Jesus has already opposed this desire for honor and privilege rather than for God's will. As before, the negative contrast between Jesus' passion predictions and the disciples' desires underscores the inauthenticity of their response.

The inauthentic responses evident in this last incident reinforce those discovered already: a refusal to attend to Jesus' words about his suffering for God's *basileia,* and a concern for personal honor while Jesus follows God's will by proclaiming the inbreaking of God's *basileia* and, consequently, nears the cross where he will suffer for freeing others. The disciples have not understood that God's way is radically different from the Way of Humanity which keeps many in bondage. Instead, the *basileia* of God for them is simply the "way things have always been" except for a new group of people in the places of honor.

Jesus' Corrective Teaching: Authentic Responses

Robert Tannehill has called attention to the key roles played by three literary devices called antithetical aphorisms in Jesus' attempts to correct the disciples' inauthentic responses. An antithetical aphorism is a brief, pointed saying that makes a strong, unqualified statement by means of a sharp contrast. The contrast is expressed in a wordplay that uses the same words in positive and negative form or which uses antithetical words.[21] The contrast in the aphorisms highlights the difference between Jesus' way for himself and his followers and common assumptions about the way the world is. They remind us of his previous teachings in parables. Through their paradoxical promises the aphorisms issue a call to disciples to follow Jesus' new way.

The first of the aphorisms occurs in 8:35, but we begin our study at 8:34. There Jesus called the crowd together with his disciples, an action opposite his usual practice of separating disciples from the crowd for teaching. Indeed, his plainly stated passion announcement (8:32) was opposite his usual teaching in parables (4:34). These unusual actions by Mark's Jesus emphasize the significance of the teaching that follows and call us to pay close attention.

Instead of rebuking the notion that the Son of man/New Human Being must suffer (as Peter had done in 8:32), Jesus expects his followers to deny themselves and take up their crosses as they follow him on his way (8:34). "Deny" here is the same word used of Peter's denial of Jesus while Jesus is on trial for his life (14:72). There Peter disassociated himself from Jesus in order to protect himself. Jesus calls, in 8:34, for the opposite response, to refuse to bend all one's energies toward preserving, protecting, and securing one's life in this world,[22] and instead to disassociate oneself from such efforts for the sake of Jesus. Indeed, the call to cross-bearing that follows implies the willingness to make any sacrifice, even life itself, for the way of the Lord. Though in our day cross-bearing has been interpreted as everything from bearing up under a difficult boss to enduring the pain of various diseases to the self-negation of which women are so often guilty, in Mark's day "cross" had only one connotation: upon it Rome executed political dissidents.[23] Jesus' call, then, to "take up the cross" is an invitation to risk the consequences of actively proclaiming God's *basileia* and its subversion of "the way things are." Again, twentieth-century Christians need only think of persons like Bonhoeffer and King to understand the contemporary implications of Jesus' invitation. Thus Jesus' teaching here demands of followers a commitment to the way of the Lord so radical that even though they know the way may lead to suffering, they follow anyway. John Zizioulas has noted that early Christian spirituality was based on accepting the way of the crucified Son of man/New Human Being so that from its earliest days it was never an uncostly spirituality.[24] Verse 34 affirms such a costly spirituality as an authentic spirituality for Mark.

The antithetical aphorism enters the story at 8:35 to expound Jesus' call in 8:34. The words used in positive and negative fashion to create the paradox are "save" and "lose." Why would someone embrace a costly spirituality? Because those who would save their life will lose it, but those who lose it for the sake of Jesus and the gospel will save it.

The aphorism directs us toward the future. Saving the present life by avoiding martyrdom means losing it in the life to come; letting go of the present life by committing it to Jesus and the gospel means gaining life in the *basileia* of God when it comes in power. The future-oriented sayings that follow in verses 8:38 and 9:1 add weight to the aphorism. The Son of man/New Human Being who suffers and dies but is raised will come again in glory, but he will be ashamed of those who were ashamed of him and his words (8:38). Consequently, these will lose their life in God's *basileia* as shown in the judgment of the evil tenants in the parable of the vineyard owner (12:9). But the positive side of this eschatology is also given: Some standing there will not die until they see that the *basileia* of God has come in power (9:1). While this verse creates its own historical and interpretive problems, its function in this context is clear. Its assurance of the coming power of God's *basileia* encourages would-be followers to commit themselves radically, even recklessly, to Jesus.

This passage affirms a strong belief in a sense of life that transcends death, a spiritual life in God, an ultimate life that is worth the radical commitment of one's present life. They remind us of what we encountered in 3:1–6: God is the God of Life. The supreme threat of political and religious elites, in Jesus' day or our own, is the power to punish by death. Where does one find the courage to face such a threat? Mark believed that faith in the ultimate life that God promises gives this courage. Earthly powers may kill, but they cannot destroy the *life* God gives. Faithful persons, therefore, continue to proclaim the inbreaking of God's *basileia* as Jesus did despite threats and thereby expose the evil of oppressive powers.[25] At present this life in God is hidden and unavailable to our human senses (borrowing language from 4:21–25). At present authentic followers of Jesus have only the eyes and ears of their radical faith that enable them to "see" and "hear" the truth of God in Jesus' words and actions so that they accept Jesus' invitation to self-denial and cross-bearing.

After Jesus discovered the disciples discussing among themselves who was the greatest (9:34), he called them together to teach them what he expected in place of their desire for honor. He used another antithetical aphorism: "If anyone wishes to be first, let that one be last of all and servant of all" (9:35). Then he acted out a parable to show what he meant: he received a child, placed it in the midst of them, even took the child in his arms. A child in Mark's world was a helpless, insignificant part of an adult-oriented culture, one of those at the bottom of the pecking order without honor for herself or himself. Thus a child was least able to reward attention granted to it with any recognizable greatness or honor.[26] Jesus' reception of the child underscores his expectation that, instead of seeking honor, his followers will choose to serve all persons, especially children and other least ones. He reaffirms this teaching later after the disciples tried to keep children from him (10:13). Indignantly he told them, "Let the children come to me, do not stop them, for to such as these is the *basileia* of God" (10:14). The acted parable, along with these words, thus reveals another means of self-denial and another authentic response: Since a child has no honor with which to reward service to himself or herself, performance of such service requires letting go of any claim of power over lesser ones as well as the desire for honor from peers and replacing it with compassion for all.

Obviously the word "receive" in 9:37 means more than perfunctory acceptance. In an act of prophetic realism Jesus took the child totally to himself and identified himself with the small, honorless, powerless ones.[27] He calls his disciples to do the same. The service they render is not to be a patronizing helping hand but to identify with the lowliest ones. The disciples' reward is that in so doing they receive both Christ (instead of greater honor from people), who has identified himself with the little ones, and God who sent this Christ to us (9:37). The promised reward highlights the authenticity of this response. Thus Mark's Jesus has given the saying about first and last and service (9:35) a mystical significance. Where is God? For those looking through eyes of faith, God will be "seen" and served in these lowly, powerless ones. When we identify with and receive them, we find God. Jesus has again challenged the assumptions of the values of his society in a fundamental way and revealed the new way authentic followers are to go.

The final antithetical aphorism follows the previously noted discussion between Jesus, James, John, and the others of the Twelve about obtaining positions of power and honor in the future glory of Jesus (10:35–40). Jesus begins his correction this time by describing the way power is exercised in the present world. The rulers of the Gentiles, he claimed, "lord over" them (10:42). The Greek word for "lord over" has the sense of "power over others," the use of authority for the advantage and privilege of the rulers to the disadvantage and oppression of the ruled.[28] The inauthenticity of this type of exercise of power is made clear in Jesus' charge, "It is not thus among you" (10:43a). Instead, Jesus insists, "Whoever wishes to become great among you will be the servant of you, and whoever wishes to be first among you will be slave of all" (10:43b–44).

To understand Jesus' teaching here we must first note that he presupposes a community of followers, as he did in 7:1–30 where he laid the foundation for inclusiveness in that community. His gospel is not a matter only of an individual soul. To follow Jesus means to enter a movement, to become a member of God's people who are on the way to the cross and beyond to God's glory.[29] Second, we must see that he calls for this community to practice the discipleship of equals. The contrast Jesus describes in these verses is not between two ways of exercising power over others, a good way versus a bad way, but between any power over others and service.[30] No "lording over," no structures of domination are to to be tolerated. These are inauthentic responses as Jesus taught the disciples. He makes the same point in two other places in Mark. In 3:34–35 he declares, "Whoever does the will of God, this one is my brother and sister and mother." In 10:29–31 he insists that those who leave house, family, or lands will receive "now in this time houses and brothers and sisters and mothers and children and lands with persecutions and, in the age to come, eternal life." In both declarations "fathers," the ones who wielded the power and had highest status in the ancient patriarchal family, are conspicuously absent.

There is no room for the exercise of patriarchal power in this new family wherein all forms of domination and subordination are rejected. Instead, true leadership in this community is rooted in service to and solidarity with each other.[31] Here is yet another means of self-denial, for honor from God is received for doing that which people considered dishonorable: acting as slaves and servants of one another. Significantly, even Jesus never exercises power over another person in Mark's story. He commanded nature (e.g., 4:39) and demons (e.g., 9:25), but he exhorts, urges, warns human beings without controlling them.[32] Therefore, service and solidarity are authentic responses to the call of Christ who served humanity by ransoming its bondage at great cost to himself (10:45).

Summary of Mark
8:31–9:1; 9:30–37; 10:32–45

One of God's initiatives in these passages was found to be the giving of Christ as a ransom for freeing people from the things that bind and oppress them (e.g., the purity system, honor, demonic powers). The result of Jesus' offer of his life as a ransom is that people are enabled to live as God intended in God's *basileia*. The second divine initiative gleaned from these texts is God's revelation that the way into the freedom of God's *basileia* leads inevitably through suffering for the sake of the gospel. This suffering is not a catastrophe suggesting the power and victory of evil. Instead it accomplishes the will of God who through Jesus is subverting the world as people have known it.

The authentic responses to God's initiatives may be gathered together under the heading "imitation of Christ." The relationship between Jesus' predictions of his own passion and his teaching to his disciples reveals that the role of Jesus and that of his followers are coordinate.[33] Followers are to imitate Jesus' understanding of suffering for the *basileia* of God as the inevitable result of subverting the world as is and thus accomplishing God's will. Authentic followers subvert the world because they identify with the least ones in society, choose to be slaves and servants of all, and seek no position of power or honor for themselves atop an old pecking order but practice the discipleship of equals in the community of Jesus' followers. Authentic disciples understand and embrace this new way of Jesus even at great cost to themselves.

Together these responses teach us what Jesus meant by the call to deny self. He did not call us to self-negation, the attitude that causes one to view oneself as an emptiness without value to peers or to God. This type of self-negation is mostly characteristic of women who have been socialized to submerge themselves in others' identities, needs, and interests (usually fathers, husbands, or children) and thus never admit their own needs or develop their own God-given gifts. It can lead to triviality, distractability, dependence on others, inability to make decisions for oneself, mistrust of reason, fear, self-hatred, jealousy, timidity.[34] These characteristics are hardly those of authentic disciples of Christ who courageously stand against the oppressions of their world by choosing not to pursue their own greatness or secure their own lives, but decide instead to practice the discipleship of equals among those who follow Jesus who identified with an honorless child, came to serve others, and gave his life as a ransom for many.

The community of mothers, brothers, sisters, and children (no fathers, for this is not a patriarchal household) is one reward in the present life promised to authentic followers by Mark's Jesus (10:30). A second reward is that Christ and God will be found in the least ones with whom they identify and whom they serve. Jesus also promised that there will be vindication for his persecuted followers, but vindication is not promised in this present life. Instead it comes at the end when the Son of man/New Human Being—the same one who suffered and died but who was raised to life—comes in power and glory to usher his followers into the Life of God. We will see more on this subject in the discussion of Mark 13.

The inauthentic responses to God can also be summarized under one heading: refusal to imitate Christ in his suffering and service to others. Followers of the Way of Humanity instead seek privilege, honor, and greatness in this life. Rather than denying self and taking up the cross, they are bent on self-preservation. They cannot accept that suffering for the gospel accomplishes God's will. They wish to be served rather than serve and suffer for others. Thus they cause suffering through their oppression of those forced to serve them. They have no concern for the least ones while they compete with peers for positions of honor. They do not understand that Jesus' new way is not about changing who is at the top of the pecking order but about ending pecking orders altogether, with their dominating and subjugating forms of leadership. They would certainly be ashamed to follow a suffering, servant Messiah. The inauthenticity of their responses will be made clear to them when the Son of man/New Human Being comes in his glory and is ashamed of them (8:38).

Mark 13:1–37

Farewell speeches dealing with the future are commonly attributed to great leaders in the Bible near the end of their lives. The speeches of Jacob (Gen. 49), Moses (Deut. 32), and David (1 Chron. 28) are examples. John's Gospel has an account of such a speech from Jesus at the Last Supper (John 14—17). Not surprisingly, therefore, Mark also records Jesus making a farewell address (13:1–37). It concludes the section of the Gospel wherein the religious leaders resume their major role in the story as the confrontation between them and Jesus intensifies (11:1–13:37). The primary spatial location for this section of Mark is the Temple, the seat and symbol of the religious leaders' power. There Jesus is challenged by his enemies (11:27–33; 12:13–27). There he confronts them (12:1–12, 35–40) and curses the Temple system for what it had come to be (11:12–25; see chapter 5). As Jesus leaves the Temple for the last time at 13:1, one of his disciples comments on its beauty. He responds by pronouncing its coming destruction (v. 2) and then sits down opposite it on the Mount of Olives to deliver his farewell speech (v. 3). The following address shows the result (the Temple's destruction), according to Mark's Jesus, of the leadership's refusal to receive his proclamation of God's *basileia*. As will be seen, the Temple's destruction also prepares the way for the apocalyptic tone of the discourse.

Connecting devices and repeated themes throughout chapter 13 indicate Mark's intent to present a coherent, unified discourse.[35] Traditional apocalyptic motifs are present—wars, earthquakes, plagues, and famine herald the imminent end of history (vv. 7–8). Indeed, Mark follows an apocalyptic perspective that sees history moving toward its ultimate goal according to the specific plan of God, culminating in the coming of the Son of man/New Human Being (v. 26). Furthermore, Mark makes use of the "poetry" of apocalyptic language which is designed to open up possibilities rather than limit them, to evoke rather than define meanings. While many things make people look, poetry, along with other artistic expressions, enables us to "see." Thus apocalyptic language elicits emotions, reactions, and convictions that cannot be phrased in propositional–logical language. Instead, the evocative power of apocalyptic's poetic descriptions invites readers' imaginative participation so that they can "see" the vision that is narrated.[36] But in the midst of all this apocalyptic material, Mark also edits the material in such a way that he softens apocalyptic speculations.[37] Instead of intense conjecture about the end, a hortatory interest is present in the discourse. The "when" of the disciples' initial question ("When will these things be?" v. 4) is bypassed in favor of exhortation: Mark's Jesus utters eighteen imperatives in the discourse. Indeed, his words are a prophecy of the destruction of the Temple and the coming of the end of time. They work equally well, however, as a challenge to his disciples.[38] Thus we are given a fine opportunity in this discourse to grasp how Mark felt his community should respond while awaiting the fulfillment of God's purposes.

God's Initiative

"But *you* see! I have told you everything beforehand"—these words of Mark's Jesus in 13:23 indicate God's initiative in this discourse. Apocalyptic groups often claimed to have exclusive revelation of the secrets of God's purposes which were revealed to them by an intermediary from God. Because of these secrets such groups could assert confidently God's ultimate control over the future even when present history appeared chaotic and out of control. In 13:23 Jesus, functioning as the intermediary of God's *basileia,* tells his followers that he is revealing in advance the end of all things which God has ordained, what the signs of the end are (and are not), and how they are to respond to this revelation in the present. We will discuss details of this revelation in the following sections, but at this point we can see that once again the initiative God has taken is to reveal significant "mysteries" through Jesus to those who would be God's people.

The Responses in
the Exhortation Sections

R. H. Lightfoot outlined the discourse in Mark 13 in a manner that is helpful for organizing study of the responses to God's initiative.

13:5–13	The Beginning of the Consummation
13:14–27	The Consummation Itself
13:28–37	Warnings in Connection with the Consummation[39]

The seventeen imperatives that Jesus announces occur in every division of the outline (vv. 5, 7, 9, 11, 14, 15, 15, 16, 18, 21, 23, 28, 29, 33, 33, 35, 37). Since imperatives indicate responses sought by a speaker, our search for authentic and inauthentic responses to God's initiative will focus on Jesus' imperatives. The ones contained in the first and third sections of the outline, which are sections of exhortation, will be examined first. Study of the second section, which gives details regarding the coming of the Son of man/New Human Being, will follow.

Having pronounced destruction on the Temple (v. 2), Jesus sat down opposite it on the Mount of Olives, where his four prominent disciples (see 1:16–20) asked him, "Speak to us, when will these things be, and what is the sign when all these things are about to be completed?" (v. 4). As earlier Mark has recorded a double question (see 7:5) to broaden a discussion that began with the destruction of the Temple so that it includes a wider subject: observations about the end of history. The double question suggests that, at least for some of Mark's readers, the ruination of the Temple was linked to the consummation of history.[40] So, while the disciples' question connects Mark 13 to the preceding events in the Gospel that were set in the Temple (chs. 11—12), it also sets the apocalyptic tone of the speech that follows.

The first imperative occurs in verse 5 as the discourse proper begins: "*See* that someone does not deceive you!" The imperative is reminiscent of 4:24 where Jesus commanded the disciples, "See what you hear!" Once again followers of Jesus are called to be perceptive, to see beyond surface appearances. The ones who would deceive them are messianic pretenders proclaiming, "I am he" (v. 6), and those claiming that wars and rumors of such, earthquakes, and famines (vv. 7–8) are signs that the end is at hand. The word of Mark's Jesus is that these events are "the beginning of the birthpangs" (v. 8), but the end is not yet (v. 7). Since he is revealing this truth beforehand, the authentic response is to "see through" the words of pretenders when they come and thus not to be deceived by their calculations of the "when" of the end.

Jesus commands them also, "Do not fear!" (v. 7). They are not to fear because Jesus has told them that these birthpangs are inevitable parts (that word "must" again) of the divine plan (v. 7) which is being worked out even through these troubles. In the midst of upheaval and suffering, people often fear that God is not present, that God has abandoned them, that history is random after all. Mark's Jesus seeks to quell such fear by assuring followers beforehand that God is present and at work even in the midst of suffering. God is now in the process of bringing about the divine purpose in history. Since Jesus has given them advance notice, authentic followers are able to "see" God's presence and purpose even in chaos and, therefore, not be afraid.

At verse 9, as the scene shifts from global strife (vv. 7–8) to circumstances specifically involving God's people, Jesus repeats the command, "See!" This time, however, the command is, "See yourselves." Perhaps this command carries the sense of, "Know what you are really about," since he warns them that they will be handed over to authorities and beaten in the synagogues (v. 9). Thus, just as the appearance of Christ in glory is bound up with his suffering and death (8:31–38), so disciples' hope in God's ultimate victory must survive their suffering at the hands of religious and political powers. Already Jesus has charged that those without deep roots of faith will not endure persecution on account of the word (4:17). Jesus' command in verse 9 is a call to authentic followers to see themselves, to know that they have the deep faith that will ready them for the suffering that is coming.

Verse 9 concludes with the note that disciples' arrests and trials will be an opportunity for bearing witness to the gospel, which is significant since the gospel must be preached to all nations first (v. 10). The simple word "first" throws more cold water on the fires of intense apocalyptic speculation. As Mark wrote, the gospel had obviously not been preached to all nations, so any current events could not be signs that the end was at hand. Meanwhile, rather than forsaking their faith in the midst of persecution, disciples must continue to proclaim the gospel everywhere. Thus, Mark's Jesus has interpreted a negative situation in a positive way. What could have appeared meaningless (being persecuted for their faith) actually has great significance since it creates an opportunity to participate in the hastening of the end by proclaiming the gospel before those who judge. When we remember that in the Second Gospel Jesus "preaches" not only with his words but also by his actions, then we know the same should be true for disciples as they are called to proclaim the gospel to all nations.

This is a good time to ask, What does Mark consider to be the "good news," the gospel that must be proclaimed to all nations? What have we uncovered thus far? God empowered Jesus through the Spirit to announce that God's *basileia* has drawn near (1:9–15). We have seen in Mark's story that under the reign of God, people are freed from whatever binds them by Jesus' teachings and miracles and also by his death, which is understood as a ransom for many, as an exodus from slavery. All people—not race, class, ethnicity, gender, age, or physical condition count against a person since God looks at the heart—are received and valued by God and taught to value one another as members of a new inclusive "family" that practices the discipleship of equals. Thus Mark's Gospel is good news for those who have found themselves in bondage (of whatever kind).

Mark's Gospel is bad news, however, for those who want to maintain their privilege, power, and status over others. How are disciples able to maintain their proclamation in the midst of persecution at the hands of those in power and while on trial for their faith? Verse 11 promises supernatural aid for disciples in this endeavor. The Holy Spirit will speak through them, aiding them in their witness. Thus disciples are commanded not to be anxious but to speak whatever is given to them in that hour, trusting that the words come from the Spirit whom God has promised them. Lack of anxiety, trust in God's promised help through the Spirit, and speaking whatever is given to them to say are authentic responses to Jesus' command to bear witness to all nations.

As the proclamation spreads, the "worst of the End-time woes"[41] will occur. Families will turn on those members who follow Jesus

(v. 12), and people will hate disciples (v. 13a). But the one who endures to the end will be saved (v. 13b). Elisabeth Schüssler Fiorenza has suggested translating the Greek word for "endure" as "consistently resist," meaning disciples should continually resist efforts to stop their proclamation by those opposed to God's liberating *basileia*.[42] We have already recalled Mark 4:16–17, which noted that those with a rootless faith are unable to endure (or resist) persecution on account of the word. The opposite response—the authentic response of those who "see" themselves and have allowed the word to be planted deeply in their hearts, who do not get anxious but trust in God's help and allow the Spirit to speak through them—is to persevere in their faith even when persecuted. Then, whenever the end may come, they will be saved.

Immediately following the parousia section (vv. 14–27) comes the metaphor of the fig tree with the imperative "learn": "From the fig tree *learn* the parable" (v. 28). The first budding of the fig tree gives an unerring sign of the arrival of spring when the dead of winter is over. Just so, the disciples must *know* (another imperative, v. 29) in their own sufferings for God's *basileia* the unerring sign of the approach of the Son of man/New Human Being who is near, even at the gates (v. 29b). He is so near that "this generation" will not pass away before all these things happen (v. 30). By using the "poetry" of apocalyptic language Mark's Jesus does not so much fix a precise date for the end as fill the hearers' every present moment with a sense of urgency, for just at this point he also asserts that the exact time of the end is not known by anyone but God (v. 32). Thus in this one discourse Mark's Jesus rejects the false eschatological timetable of some people (vv. 5–8) but seeks to retain a sense of the urgency regarding his return (vv. 30–32).[43] So, know that he is near, and because he is near, suffering for his sake, proclamation of the gospel to all nations, and perseverance in faith matter greatly.

The two imperatives that follow in verse 33 should be understood in light of both the sense of urgency in verse 30 and the warning against false timetables in verse 32. The first imperative is one encountered before: "See!" It links the parable of the servants in the house of the absent lord (vv. 34–37) to the same command to see beyond surface appearances in previous passages of Mark. The second imperative is, "Be alert," or "Be awake!" The Greek word indicates a call not to be surprised or unprepared, not to be caught off guard, not to be insensitive to the situation at hand.[44] Thus disciples are called to "see" and be alert for Christ's return in the same way that servants in the house of an absent lord must "see" that the lord could return at any time (they do not know when, v. 35) and thus be always alert and about their work (v. 34). Their "work" is the mission given them by the lord.

In many ways this parable about an absentee lord and his servants is an untimely choice by Jesus who has called his followers to form a community without these types of hierarchical (and therefore, oppressive) relationships. But clearly the parable's placement in this discourse shows that disciples' "work" is faithfulness amid persecutions and trials so that they continue proclaiming the gospel until it reaches all nations. Verse 35 repeats the command to be alert. Unfortunately Jesus' disciples demonstrate the inauthentic responses to Jesus' command. Though they promised to remain steadfast no matter the cost (14:29, 31), they slept in Gethsemane as Jesus prayed for the ability to endure (14:34–42), then fled when Jesus' opponents came for him (14:43–50). They were unprepared and caught off guard so that they bore no witness on Jesus' behalf. The opposite responses of seeing, being alert, and being about the mission of proclaiming the gospel are authentic ones to the revelation Jesus gave that God will consummate history according to the divine plan. Thus every moment is transformed and renewed in the light of God's future for those alert to it, for any moment may become the very one in which Christ returns.[45]

The final imperative of the discourse is a repetition of "Be alert!" (v. 37), this time given not only to the four disciples present with Jesus but to the whole community for which Mark was writing ("what I say to you I say to all"). Here is the final word of the speech, the last command of Jesus before the narrative of his suffering begins in Mark 14: Be alert! The authenticity of being alert, of not being caught off guard by suffering, is sharply emphasized.

The Responses in the Parousia Section

Between the promise in verse 13 that the one persevering to the end will be saved and the final two parables of the discourse that emphasize alertness and watchfulness while awaiting the end (vv. 28–37) is a description of the return of Christ itself (vv. 14–27). From its Jewish roots Christianity inherited the transcendental, apocalyptic faith that looked for God's presence at the end of history. Christians looked for the meaning of life in the final act of God from which all present and past events receive their explanation and significance.[46] To seek meaning in this final act of God is to find a means of coping with the present suffering of the righteous, for an apocalyptic faith hoped for a reversal of the human condition, including vindication of the righteous, soon.[47] Through their use of evocative language, Christian apocalypticists seek to enable readers to "see" that God is at work bringing history to its final moment, which in Mark would be Christ's return, despite surface appearances suggesting that evil and chaos control the world (as frequently appears to be the case today!). In this hope disciples find courage to resist persecution and continue their proclamation of the gospel.

In the discourse prior to verse 14 the message of Mark's Jesus has been, "See, persevere, do not be afraid, trust God, keep proclaiming the gospel because the end is not yet." Verse 14, however, paints a portrait of the time when the waiting is over. The sign of this time is the abomination of desolation standing where he ought not.[48] In an unusual direct address to the reader ("let the reader understand!" v. 14), Mark himself insists that disciples note the full power of Jesus' words. The poetic language that follows evokes the significance of this time when God will bring history to its fulfillment: When this sign occurs disciples must act immediately. Those in Judea must flee to the hill country; there is no refuge in the holy city. The flight is so urgent that a person must not go down or enter the house or turn back from the fields (vv. 15–16; these commands are three more of the imperatives of the discourse). Verses 17 and 18 show compassion for those fleeing from a terrible destruction—it is bad for mothers with children; pray (another imperative) that it does not happen in winter. Verse 19 continues the traditional apocalyptic language by which Mark's Jesus describes an unprecedented time of suffering that God, because of the chosen ones, curtails. The description of God's merciful intervention (v. 20) promises disciples that the distress will not outlast their powers of endurance.

There is another warning against messianic deceivers, but the situation in verse 21 is different from that in verse 6. The description now is of the time to expect the end and the coming of Christ so that the danger of being deceived by pretenders is especially great.[49] The new specific warning is not to be deceived by those performing signs and wonders (v. 22). We have already seen that Jesus announced a *basileia* of God that was hidden but surely present in his words, work, and destiny. There are no showy displays (see 8:11–12). External proofs and rationalistic certainty are not God's way. Jesus' followers must, therefore, not be deceived by those putting on shows. Instead they must see (v. 23a; note vv. 5, 9, 33) what God is bringing about, which is the end that God has ordained, the end that Jesus has told them about beforehand (v. 23b).

They will see if they are using eyes of faith that God's *basileia* does not remain hidden (note 4:22). Jesus describes disruptions in the heavens (vv. 24–25) that precede the moment when everyone "will see the Son of man/New Human Being coming in the clouds with much power and glory" (v. 26). The clouds, which commonly manifest the glory of God (see Ex. 34:5), unveil Jesus' hitherto hidden glory so that he is seen by all. He takes on God's function of gathering together the elect, scattered people of God (v. 27): those who have borne witness to Jesus before all nations; who have been hated and persecuted for Jesus' sake but persevered in their proclamation; who saw God at work even in the chaos around them and thus kept alert to the fulfillment that God was bringing about. The promise to them is that Christ will gather them together to share in his glory. Their vindication is certain.

This description of the coming of the Son of man/New Human Being is intended to encourage disciples suffering for the gospel. The poetic language empowers authentic disciples to experience (imaginatively) the coming of the Son of man/New Human Being which brings glory not only for Christ but also for his faithful ones. It enables them to see that their present suffering for God's *basileia* is part of a history over which God is Lord and which is being brought to fulfillment, though the suffering ones do not know how (remember 4:26–29). Inauthentic responses include not only falling away when facing persecution for the gospel but also being deceived by those claiming to know the when of the end. As Eugene Petersen has pointed out, those who read apocalyptic literature only as a predictive word are procrastinating, putting distance between themselves and the application of the vision, putting off dealing with it until some future date. The revelation of what will happen soon (Christ is "near, at the very gates," v. 29) should mean precisely that. It will happen as soon as hearts are responsive, as soon as ears hear and eyes see that God is at work in the world even now, as soon as mouths proclaim that this is so.[50]

Summary of Mark 13:1–37

The God who is experienced in Mark 13 is one who is Lord of history and is at work, though that work is presently hidden except to eyes of faith, bringing history to the fulfillment God has planned when God's people will be gathered together and vindicated. Furthermore, God takes the initiative to reveal this fulfillment through Jesus to God's faithful people so that they may know of its sure coming and, thus, find encouragement to endure suffering on behalf of the gospel.

Authentic responses to this God begin (again) with true seeing that looks beyond surface appearances so that disciples are not deceived by those who claim that the signs say the end is at hand. In particular they must see through messianic pretenders and false prophets who seek to deceive by misinterpreting events that are taking place or are about to take place. They must listen only to Jesus who has told them all things beforehand. The evocative language of Jesus' apocalyptic message portrays the Son of man/New Human Being as near, even at the gates. But Mark's Jesus also reminds followers that God alone knows when the end will come, a statement that appears to be lost on both the writers and readers of contemporary best-sellers claiming to predict the when of the end. The details in Mark call authentic disciples to be ever alert, to have every present moment transformed by a sense of urgency about Christ's return. The Last Supper in Mark reinforces this call to alertness, for it is celebrated by taking the cup in anticipation of the day when it will be drunk anew in the *basileia* of God (14:22–25). Thus the inauthentic responses so far take two forms: (1) being too concerned about the when of the end which can lead to efforts to calculate the date, being deceived by false prophets and messianic pretenders who claim to have made such calculations, or putting off dealing with God's purpose until some future date; or (2) being unconcerned about the end and, therefore, not alert to its urgency, reality, or nearness.

While awaiting Christ's return, disciples are given work to do—the proclamation of the gospel to all nations. The authentic response is to be at this work when the Lord returns. The life of the community in the present age is thus of paramount importance: only as it remains faithful in its witness to the gospel even during persecution will Jesus' liberating message go forth. Furthermore, disciples are expected not to be anxious about this proclamation, even when it is in the form of testimony before a tribunal, because they trust God to give the Holy Spirit to speak through them.

In addition to these other authentic responses, disciples are to see themselves so that they know their roots of faith are deep. Consequently, when suffering for God's *basileia* comes they do not fall away. Before this discourse they were told that suffering for the gospel is inevitable (8:31, 34). They must persevere through this suffering to the end. They must not fear, for they have been told beforehand that their suffering will be vindicated. These too are authentic responses to the God who has a plan for history. Mark, in the style of a true apocalyptic spirituality, envisioned that God would indeed intervene on behalf of God's own who were suffering. That intervention will occur, however, at the culmination of history when Christ will appear, unveil the heretofore hidden purpose of God for history, and gather the elect. This vindication for disciples will be definitive. So, authentic spirituality from this perspective calls for perseverance and a vigilant expectation of the Lord's coming to ask for an account of God's servants' deeds and to reward those who have been faithful to the end to Christ's gospel.

The inauthentic responses here are obvious: lack of faith that God is in control of history and will ultimately vindicate the elect, and fear of suffering for Christ's sake so that would-be disciples fall away before persecution on account of the word (see 4:16–17) and do not continue to bear witness to the gospel.

Chapter 5

Responding to the God of Life, Power, Judgment, and Prayer

Our study in chapter 4 focused on Jesus' teachings in the second half of Mark, so in this chapter we turn to Jesus' miracles. Thus we complete the examination of Jesus' "teaching with deeds" begun in chapter 3.

Mark 9:14–29

The healing of the so-called epileptic boy occurs, like the passion prediction patterns, in the part of Mark where events take place "on the way." This section is organized around Jesus' journey to Jerusalem, a journey that should be understood spiritually as well as literally. On the way Jesus teaches and prepares disciples for the passion that lies ahead. Emphasis falls on Jesus' approaching suffering and death and how disciples should respond to those events. Thus there are few displays of Jesus' power, unlike the first half of the Gospel. As a result, the exorcism of 9:14–29 stands out in sharp relief.

The introductory verse (14) is generally considered to be Mark's composition,[1] which suggests he is responsible for placing this story in this place, perhaps as a foil to the transfiguration (9:2–9). We see the same Jesus who was glorified on the mountain once more at work among ordinary people on the plain below. Also noteworthy is the significant interplay between life and death in the discussion following the transfiguration (9:10–13), and in the miracle story that concerns us in 9:14–29. We will see how this interplay influences Mark's hopes for disciples.

In addition to its placement, Mark's editing of the story sheds light on what he hoped readers would "see." By means of his introduction in verse 14 ("and having come to the disciples") and his conclusion in which the disciples ask for and receive private explanation of their failure (as in 4:10–13; 7:18–23),[2] Mark has brought the responses of disciples to the forefront. Plus, the private explanation they are given is interesting in itself. ⟨Its focus is prayer⟩ The story it concludes, however, centers on faith. Had Mark merely wanted to continue the emphasis on faith, he knew a tradition to use: 11:22–23, the one Matthew chose (Matt. 17:20).[3] Mark's decision, then, to emphasize at the end the disciples' responses and also prayer appears to be deliberate and calls for close attention, especially in this study of Markan spirituality.

The result of Mark's editing of tradition is a story that may be diagrammed as follows:

A   9:14–18   Disciples' Failure
  B   9:19–20   The Boy and the Crowd
    C   9:21–24   Conversation between Jesus and the Father
  B'   9:25–27   The Boy and the Crowd
A'   9:28–29   Disciples' Failure[4]

In addition to giving attention to disciples' responses and the prayer teaching Mark has added, our study should also take note of the conversation between Jesus and the father. The memorable, haunting cry of the father in verse 24, "I believe; help my unbelief," is the center of the story as Mark has recorded it. By contrast, Matthew and Luke relate this event without the dialogue between Jesus and the father. For those two evangelists Jesus' miracle was the center of the story (see Matt. 17:14–21; Luke 9:37–42). Mark, however, was keenly interested in the faith and prayers of those who were acquainted with Jesus' power.

This miracle story, therefore, is significant for a study of Markan spirituality because of its placement "on the way" and its concern for faith and prayer. Furthermore, we cannot lose sight of its being an exorcism and will examine its significance in the analysis of God's initiative that follows.

God's Initiative

In a climactic moment in the story, Mark relates that Jesus rebuked a demon who was tormenting a boy, and the demon came out of him at Jesus' word. This exorcism is hardly the first in Mark's Gospel. It's not even the first one examined in this study (remember 7:24–30). As many scholars have noted, the victory of the Spirit of God in Jesus over the demonic spirits is a major theme of Mark's witness to Jesus.[5] Interpretation of 7:24–30 did not require extensive consideration of demon-possession. Such is not the case with this story.

The theme of the Spirit of God versus the demonic spirits begins early in Mark. After being baptized by water and the Spirit, Jesus was compelled by the Spirit into the wilderness to be assailed by Satan (1:9–13). Following that confrontation he announced that the *basileia* of God has drawn near (1:14–15). Then the first miracle that Mark reports is an exorcism in a synagogue (1:21–28). Mark's intention in these early verses is clear: Jesus is the agent of God's *basileia* come to defeat the demonic powers opposed to God. Thus the exorcisms reveal the power of God's Holy Spirit at work in Jesus to defeat the unholy spirits. This power is highlighted in the story being considered here by the emphatic pronoun used in his rebuke: "*I* command you, come out of him!" (9:25). The stronger one has indeed come (1:7; 3:27), and the *basileia* of God has begun to replace the oppressive rule of Satan. Consequently, exorcisms were central to Jesus' mission in Mark. It is noteworthy, therefore, that God's initiative in this story to intervene miraculously "on the way" to Jerusalem, one of only two times God so acts in this section of Mark, is to exorcise an unclean spirit.

We should be reminded at this point of the ancient worldview that scholars have called the primordial tradition (discussed in chapter 2). Believing in both a visible, material world and a nonmaterial, spiritual world that can intersect each other allowed for belief in demons/unclean spirits as well as for belief in a Holy Spirit. Stories of demon-possession and exorcisms, therefore, can be expected from first-century writers. In addition, some scholars maintain that these stories not only reflect a worldview or relate an actual event from Jesus' ministry but also serve a highly symbolic function within the narrative. For example, an exorcism account that readily lends itself to a symbolic reading is Mark 5:1–21. The demon's name Legion (a Latin word for a division of Roman soldiers), along with other military terms in the story, suggests that the demon is symbolic of the Roman military occupation of Palestine and all its evil consequences.[6] Jesus' opposition to and defeat of such a demon would have been a welcome story for Mark's readers.

But what are twentieth-century Westerners, who usually live within a scientific worldview that is skeptical of demons, to do with such stories? Some claim to have no trouble accepting the reality of demons and the historicity of the exorcisms. Others demythologize the story so that the exorcism in 9:14–29, for example, is merely the cure of epilepsy. Still others dismiss the stories as so much unenlightened first-century superstition.[7] None of these approaches, however, addresses the socio-literary function of the exorcisms, including 9:14–29, within Mark's story. Furthermore, they leave many readers, myself included, oddly dissatisfied with their easy acceptance or easy dismissal of demons. Therefore I propose the following two-part alternative: (1) we should not neglect to appreciate the power[8] of these long-remembered stories and their impact on Mark's narrative; (2) Westerners who are no longer closed to the possibility of a spiritual reality—a burgeoning worldwide interest in spirituality suggests there are many such people[9]—can take advantage of the work of scholars who point to the symbolism in these stories and "see" demons as representative of the evil that threatens life as God intended it. While we may not all be comfortable with the idea of demons, such things as ethnic cleansing in Bosnia and Rwanda, the gang rape and beating of a Central Park jogger, the bombing-murder of 168 people (including nineteen children) in an Oklahoma City federal building, the persistence of racism and sexism, convince many of us that evil as a dehumanizing power not under our control exists in our world and needs to be "exorcised."[10] With this type of approach in mind, we can examine our story closely.

What particular nuances does Mark cast on this exorcism? There are two. First is the description of the boy's condition. The father recounts the symptoms in verses 17b–18, 21b–22. Then Mark narrates the convulsion that overtook the boy when the demon first saw Jesus in verse 20. By emphasizing the extent of the demon's effect on the boy, Mark heightens the "miraculousness" of the act Jesus performs and stresses his power. The descriptions also set the stage for depicting the manner in which Jesus exorcises the demon, particularly by the use of the Greek verb *xeraino* to describe the boy in verse 18. We encountered the verb in 3:1 as a man's "withered" hand and noted how it signaled the lifelessness of the man's hand. The NRSV translates it in 9:18 as "becomes rigid."[11] But in light of its suggestion of lifelessness elsewhere (3:1; 4:6; 11:20), it is fair to understand it as making the same suggestion here. In addition, in verse 22 Mark relates that the demon would throw the boy into fire and water so as to kill him. There is a sense, then, of lifelessness about the boy as a result of being possessed by this demon. Such an understanding is intensified by the details of the actual exorcism. After Jesus commanded the demon to come out, the boy was left looking like a corpse so that most people said, "He is dead" (v. 26). Jesus, however, took him by the hand and raised him up, and he arose (v. 27).[12] Thus, in the second nuance Mark casts on the miracle in this story, Jesus' actions underscore the power of God to release the death grip of demonic power and restore life. We have already noted the focus on God's life-giving power in 3:1–6. These are not the only two such stories in Mark. The raising of Jairus's daughter from the dead (5:41–42) has an obvious emphasis on this aspect of God's power. A later controversy with the Sadducees will find Jesus affirming, "God is not the God of the dead but of the living" (12:27). Thus, God's initiatives to use God's power to overcome evil and to give life, even where evil has apparently already wrought death, is a significant theme in Mark's Gospel and is especially highlighted in this exorcism account.

The Responses

The responses in this story begin with the disciples' inability to exorcise the demon prior to Jesus' arrival. They had seen the power of God overcome demonic forces before (see, e.g., 1:21–28, 5:1–12), and had participated with that power (6:13). They had also specifically witnessed God's life-giving power (3:1–6, 5:35–42). Therefore, it is reasonable to expect them to be able to join with God's power again to exorcise the death grip of the demon from this boy. They failed to do so, however (v. 18). The inauthenticity of this response is revealed in Jesus' cry against them: "O faithless generation! How long will I be with you? How long will I be patient with you?" (v. 19).

These words are a traditional prophetic lament (see, e.g., Deut. 32:5, 20; 1 Kings 19:14; Jer. 5:23) uttered as a divine condemnation of the whole generation to which Jesus came,[13] but the words were prompted by the disciples' failure and, therefore, pertain specifically to their action. In what way does their inability to exorcise the demon signal faithlessness? Mark does not indicate an answer until the prayer teaching he adds at the end where the disciples become players in the story again. After Jesus entered the house, the disciples asked him why they were unable to expel the demon (v. 28). Jesus answered that this kind of demon—that is, this very strong kind that brings death—cannot be driven out by anything but prayer (v. 29). The point is that successful exorcists do not make use of their own power but are dependent on the power of God.[14] There are two potential implications of Jesus' assertion. One would be that the disciples had given up on God, did not believe that God could or would intervene for them against the demonic powers that threaten death. Reading symbolically, we could say the disciples despaired that evil like the demon represented could be overcome, so they gave up and did not even pray for such.[15] Another implication might be that the disciples, perhaps in their unbelief, had in some sense relied on their own power.[16] Either or both responses lead to them being declared "faithless" by Jesus and thus are inauthentic responses to God. Believing in God's power to overcome evil and God's willingness to do so, and opening oneself to this power through prayer are the authentic responses to God as revealed by Jesus.

The response of the boy's father to the disciples' failure was to come to Jesus and ask him to help them, "If you are able" (v. 22). Jesus' reply challenges the father's uncertainty with the assertion, "All things are possible to the one who believes" (v. 23). How can all things be possible for someone? Because that someone believes in God whose power is of such magnitude that for God all things are possible. This statement is an example of an *adynaton,* an ancient literary device used to assert that an impossible action can be performed by a deity or by a human assisted by the power of this deity.[17] Similar assertions are made in 10:27 ("all things are possible with God"), 11:23–24 (to be examined next in this study), and 14:36 ("Abba, Father, all things are possible for you"). Jesus is not insisting on belief as a condition for receiving healing. Instead he calls for a sense of hopeful anticipation based on who God is—One who can do all things.[18] His words to the boy's father reinforce his teaching for disciples. Such belief, such hopeful anticipation is an authentic response to God. Uncertainty, doubt, despair, unbelief are inauthentic responses.

Some comments on the phrase "All things are possible to the one who believes" enable us to avoid misunderstanding. I begin with the rather bold statement that "all things" does not literally mean all things to Mark. I make this assertion based on the following observations of the Second Gospel. First, in Gethsemane, Jesus affirmed that all things are possible for God and asked for the cup—his suffering—to pass (14:36). But the cup did not pass and (apparently) could not if God's will was to be accomplished. Second, we have seen that disciples are promised their own suffering if they persist in pursuing God's will (8:34–37; 13:9–13). We know of many Christians, some in our own time, for whom this "prophecy" came true. Doubtlessly they and their families and friends prayed faithfully for their safety, but such was not to be. Third, despite this suffering, Mark is sure that God's will is done. He was convinced of the power of evil. He was also convinced that through the power of God people are freed from the evil that oppresses them even if their mortal lives are taken from them. Mark believed Jesus' word that evil will be finally defeated, and God's people will have the life for which they long (recall 13:26–27). Sometimes we are privileged to witness evil's defeat in our lifetimes: Someone is freed from the effects of an abusive past or overcomes an addiction, a town in Tennessee turns its back on the Klan, apartheid is ended in South Africa, and so on. But sometimes we must wait, according to Mark's Jesus, for a coming day of ultimate reckoning when God's will is fully accomplished. These observations lead me to conclude that, for Mark, "all things" actually means all those things necessary for accomplishing God's will of setting people free for the life God intended for them.[19] These things are all possible, according to Mark, because God's life-giving power is greater than the power of evil. Believing this to be true is an authentic response to God.

"I believe, help my unbelief," the father answers Jesus (v. 24). Scholars have called the father's response a half-faith or a nascent faith and note how it is plagued by hesitations, doubts, and fears that his faith is not enough to help his son. But there is also humility in the father's cry. In contrast to the disciples who tried to expel the demon by their own power, the father acknowledges his limitations and his need for God. In his doubt he does not turn away in despair but asks Jesus' help even for faith to believe in God's power to heal his son. The story of the Syrophoenician woman has already shown us that God accepts the wrestling, hurting side of humanity. Thus the father's humility, refusal to give in to despair, and awareness of his need for help are authentic responses as seen in Jesus' reaction to him. Jesus answers the cry for help by exorcising the death-dealing demon and raising up his son.[20]

Summary of Mark 9:14–29

God is experienced in this story as the God of life-giving power for whom all things necessary for achieving God's will are possible. In the story God takes the initiative through Jesus to "resurrect" the life of a boy that powerful demonic forces had sought to wither away. Now we can appreciate how the placement of this passage in Mark's story highlights this experience of God and its importance. Mark's Jesus had just announced his coming suffering (8:31). Then, on the way down from the Mount of Transfiguration during an eschatological discussion about the resurrection and Elijah, Jesus told the disciples again that he would suffer many things (9:12), and that Elijah had indeed come and "they did to him just as they wished" (v. 13), an obvious reference to John the Baptist and his fate. The following exorcism of a demon from a boy is an appropriate way to affirm resolutely the life-giving power of God that is stronger than even the death-producing power of evil. Though persons in Mark's story who oppose God and choose evil kill John and Jesus, the story of the exorcism of the boy asserts again God's power to defeat evil, free people from its death grip, and raise them to life again.

Inauthentic responses to God's initiative are narrated in the story through disciples who tried to expel the demon by their own power and failed. Though they had seen God's power restore life before, they apparently still could not "see." They did not trust God to stand with them against this evil and did not pray to God who has power over evil. Their faithlessness along with the emotions that produce it (doubt, uncertainty, despair, some of which can be seen in the possessed boy's father), their lack of prayer, and their attempts to rely on their own power are inauthentic responses to the God of life.

The authentic responses to God's life-giving power are called forth by the story. The first one is faith that is hopeful anticipation and trust in God and God's power, a power Jesus showed to be so great that it makes possible all things necessary to accomplish God's will. The second authentic response according to Mark's Jesus, then, is to turn to God in prayer for the release of that power. Prayer signals disciples' awareness of their need for God's power to defeat evil, and awareness that they need God's help even to have faith that God can and will act in the face of evil. When faith and prayer are joined, then all things necessary for evil's defeat and God's will to be done are possible for disciples because they are linked to the power of the God of life. How valuable could this good news from Mark be in a world like ours where extensive and rapid communications, not to mention our everyday lives, make us so aware of the presence of evil that yielding to despair is a strong temptation! Mark's good news offers hope that could enable us to persevere in our faith to the end.

Mark 11:12–25

The only miracle of Jesus recorded as happening in Jerusalem is the destruction of the fig tree which frames Jesus' so-called cleansing of the Temple (in Mark's Gospel it is more appropriately titled the "Cursing of the Temple" as we will see). The miracle follows the famous entry into Jerusalem (11:1–11), but the Temple, rather than all of the city, is the primary spatial location of the events in this section of Mark. In addition to the cursing event, Jesus is occupied by conflicts in the Temple with the religious leaders throughout this part of the Gospel (11:27–12:40). In 13:2 Jesus announces the Temple's coming destruction as we have seen. Thus the Temple cursing is not an isolated event but is part of the major theme of the last third of Mark, a theme that will be concluded with the ripping of the Temple veil (15:38).[21]

The cursing of the fig tree is set around the cursing of the Temple (note vv. 12–14, 20–25) by means of the observation in 11:11 that Jesus, following his entry into Jerusalem, entered the Temple, looked around, then left for the evening. Unlike Matthew and Luke, the events in the Temple will not happen until the day after the entry. On the way to the Temple on that day, Jesus encounters the fruitless fig tree. Verse 11 bears signs of Mark's composition,[22] indicating his responsibility for separating the entry into Jerusalem from the cursing of the Temple in order to make a space for the fig tree incident and create the framing effect in these verses (cf. Matt. 21:1–13; Luke 19:28–46).[23]

Such framing is a favorite Markan literary technique (see 3:20–35; 5:21–43; 6:7–30). Since framed, or intercalated, stories are to be read together, Mark intended his readers to keep the fig tree in mind while reading of the cursing of the Temple. By means of the intercalation, Mark signals that the Temple is destined for the same fate as the fig tree.

While scholars readily recognize this intercalation, there may be another not-so-obvious frame in these verses. Mark's composition allows for an outline of 11:12–25 as follows:

11:12–14	Cursing the Fig Tree
11:15–19	Cursing the Temple
11:20–21	Observation of the Dead Fig Tree
11:22–25	Observations on Prayer[24]

Sharyn Dowd has claimed that such an outline reveals a double and overlapping intercalation. The first one, the fig tree and the Temple, has a negative-negative relationship: The destruction of the fig tree parallels the destruction of the Temple. The second one, the Temple and prayer, has a negative-positive relationship: The Temple is doomed, but prayer is still operative. Just as the incident in the Temple is to be interpreted by the cursing of the fig tree (which is why we should think of the Temple being cursed rather than cleansed), so the prayer teaching is to be interpreted in light of the cursing of the Temple.[25] These considerations will prove to be important for understanding authentic and inauthentic responses to God's initiatives in this story.

God's Initiatives

In relating the odd story of the destruction of the fig tree, Mark clearly intended to describe a miracle of power. Furthermore, the accent falls on Jesus' initiative to work this miracle, for it is a peculiar one that he goes out of his way to perform. The day following the entry into Jerusalem, Jesus, traveling back to the city and the Temple, spotted a fig tree in leaf. Since he was hungry, he looked for fruit but found none because it was not the season for figs (vv. 12–13).[26] As a result, he said to it, "May no one eat fruit from you ever again" (v. 14). The verb for "eat" is in the Greek form typically used for curses, prayers, and wishes.[27] Certainly Peter interpreted Jesus' word as a curse (note v. 21). So Mark's Jesus has not merely expressed personal frustration. Instead, he has pronounced a curse or even a death sentence on the tree because of its fruitlessness.

The conclusion of the miracle is not given until the bottom of the frame in verses 20–21. There Mark tells readers that the fig tree was withered to its roots. Here again is the verb *xeraino* we saw in 3:1 and 9:18 that so strongly denotes lifelessness. Mark uses it here also to describe the power of Jesus: What he says (a death sentence) happens (the fig tree dies).

At this point readers often think there is surely more to this story than a fig tree that made Jesus mad (and unjustly so since it was not the season for figs!). What does Mark reveal about God's initiative by relating this odd miracle? Perhaps we begin to see beneath the surface of the story when we understand that figs and fig trees play significant roles in the drama of Israel that unfolds in the Hebrew Scriptures. The

fig was an emblem of peace, security, and prosperity in the golden age
of Israel's history (e.g., Deut. 8:7–8; 1 Kings 4:25). Fig trees also fig-
ure prominently in visions of Israel's future. In the messianic age, the
productivity of the earth will be prodigious, and the fig tree, with its
long season, symbolizes this prosperity (e.g., Micah 4:4; Zech. 3:10).
But the withering of the fig tree is even more often symbolic of God's
judgment on God's people or their enemies (e.g., Jer. 5:17; 8:13; Hos.
2:12; Amos 4:9). Moreover, trees are regularly employed as images of
the spiritual dimension of human beings in general and for the religious life of Israel in particular (Ps. 1:3). Where God's people are faithful, the land, and particularly the trees, flourish and bear fruit (Deut.
28). Where the people are faithless, God will visit the land with a curse
that is often actualized through the withering of the trees, especially
the vine and fig trees (e.g., Jer. 8:13).[28] The conclusion drawn from
these observations and applied to our text is that when Jesus cursed the
fig tree, he pronounced judgment on its fruitlessness. Thus one way
Mark experienced God was as judge (note 8:38).

But on what has Jesus passed judgment? A suspicion that more is
involved than the fruitlessness of a single fig tree is confirmed by
Mark's use of the fig tree story to frame the cursing of the Temple.
Since the fig tree was a symbol of the religious life of Israel, the land
should blossom and the trees bear fruit if the Temple was functioning
as it should. But the fig tree was barren, and Jesus takes the initiative
to demonstrate that the Temple was not functioning as it should. He
entered the Temple and drove out (just as he "drove out" demons; see
1:34) both those who were selling and those who were buying, overturned the seats of the money changers and those who sold doves, and
prohibited people from carrying anything through the Temple (vv.
15–16). The whole context is one of commerce, which may surprise
us today—since we usually try to separate the sacred from the secular—but would have seemed quite normal to first-century readers who
knew the Temple was the center of Palestine's redistribution economy. In such an economic system goods and services were pooled in
a central storehouse to be redistributed by the leadership to those who
needed them. In reality, the leaders made sure redistribution occurred
according to their own interests. In Palestine the central storehouse
was the Temple where an excessive burden of tributes, Temple taxes
and offerings, tithes, and other debts were collected and controlled by
the chief priestly families, elders, and Herodians, in collaboration with
Rome, of course. The merchants and money changers whom Jesus en-

countered were the "streetlevel" representatives of the economic profiteering of these religious and political elites.[29]

This system was especially difficult on the peasant population, some of whom were forced to sell their lands and even their family members into debt slavery to pay their taxes and tithes.[30] For the poorest peasants the system was devastating as illustrated by the widow who was required to give her last two copper coins to the rich Temple treasury (12:41–44). While Christians have usually read this story as a tribute to the woman's piety ("she gave all she had to God"), it is more likely in the context of Mark's world that Jesus singled her out to signal the horrific consequences of the economics of the Temple.[31] Like the demon who was taking the life of the boy in 9:14–29, the oppressive Temple system had taken the life of the widow (12:44) and others like her. No wonder a church history professor once told his class, "When religion gets sick, it gets demonic!"[32]

Jesus made clear his response to this Temple system in two ways. First, by disrupting "business," he performed a prophetic-symbolic act. More than a visual aid for a religious truth, such an act was believed to bring to pass the event portrayed.[33] Jesus' act shows that God had judged the Temple and its oppression of God's people negatively. He demonstrated physically that just as it was not the season for figs, it was no longer time for the Temple.[34]

Second, Jesus spoke God's judgment by quoting from two verses of scripture that reveal that an initiative of God has been abused. Citing Isaiah 56:7, Jesus claimed that God intended the Temple to be a house of prayer for all nations (v. 17a). Other texts from the Hebrew Scriptures affirm the Temple as the place where prayer was particularly effective (see 1 Sam. 1:1–28; 1 Kings 8:30–51; 2 Kings 19:14–37; Jonah 2:7).[35] Clearly, then, an initiative of God that Jesus valued was the giving of a place for and the privilege of prayer for all. But Jesus' use of a second verse of scripture, Jeremiah 7:11, reveals his view that God's gift of the Temple had been made into a den of robbers (v. 17b). This abuse of God's good gift made the revelation that God is the judge of evil necessary.

Finally, we should note that Mark's framing technique underscores God's power to effect God's judgment on evil. Jesus cursed the fig tree for its fruitlessness, and it withered to its roots. While the actual destruction of the Temple is not narrated in Mark's story, readers are to "see" that the Temple and its oppression is every bit as dead as the fig tree. Significantly, scholarly consensus places the writing of Mark's

Gospel between 65 and 70 C.E., either just before or just as the Romans destroyed the Temple and its leadership as a result of the Jewish revolt of 66–70 C.E.

Careful scrutiny of this passage has uncovered two initiatives of God: (1) God's gift of a place for and the privilege of prayer for all nations; (2) Jesus' revelation of God as judge of those who abuse God's good gifts for their own ends so that they oppress others and serve evil purposes. Furthermore, the text emphasizes God's power yet again, this time to effect the judgment that God pronounces.

The Responses

Which of the responses to God's initiatives does Mark displace? The first and most obviously inauthentic response is the use of the Temple for the economic and political advantage of the religious and political elites to the disadvantage of everyone else. Indeed, Jesus physically displaced this activity when he drove out those who bought and sold, and overturned the tables of the money changers and dove sellers. While these "merchants of piety"[36] had used what should have enabled access to God for all as a means to prosperity for the few, Jesus' attack suggests he considered such abuse of God's gifts to be more inauthentic than any response he had encountered. The only other time he appears to be this angry was when the religious leaders would have used the Sabbath to prevent a man's healing (3:5). What could be worse than using God's good gifts in the service of evil? Moreover, he had already taught in the parable of the sower that the desire for riches and status produce "fruitlessness." The inauthenticity of these responses could hardly be highlighted more sharply.

An indication of another inauthentic response lies in Jesus' proclamation in the Temple. In contrast to God's intent to provide a place of prayer for all stands Jesus' charge, "But *you* have made it a den of robbers" (v. 17b). The Greek word translated "robber" is distinct from the word for thief. A robber is not one who takes advantage by fiscal manipulation but one who robs by violence.[37] The implication may be that the lust for wealth in a place of extensive commercialization resulted in violent competition among the merchants which is scarcely conducive to an atmosphere favorable for prayer.

There is still more violence in this story. After Jesus had prophesied the destruction of the Temple, the religious leaders responded by plotting to destroy him (v. 18). We can note that violence is an exercise of "power over" others, an effort to get what one wants by force. Mark's Jesus has already called followers away from the use of power over others (10:41–45). He will practice his own preaching when he refuses to respond to the violence done to him with violence (see 14:46–50; 15:1–39). Thus we see in his words in the Temple and in the contrast between his and the leadership's responses to opposition that exercising power over others generally and using violence in particular are inauthentic responses to God.

In addition, Mark has shaped his story so that readers can see that death, literally or figuratively, is the result of the demonic forces at work in this world (recall 3:1–6 and 9:14–29). By contrast, God is the God of Life (as we saw in 3:1–6 and 9:14–29; also 8:31–9:1 and 13:24–27 paint this picture of God as do 5:35–43 and 12:18–27). When the religious leaders choose not to heed Jesus' words in the Temple but to plot his death instead, they show themselves to have taken the side of evil. Obviously, this response is as inauthentic here as it was at 3:6. Furthermore, the text says they wanted to kill him for fear of him because the whole crowd was spellbound by his teaching (v. 18). Does their reaction indicate envy? Indeed, Mark later tells us that the religious leaders were acting out of envy (15:10). We have seen that envy makes a heart unclean (7:22). Here we see just how unclean, how violent and evil, an envious heart can be.

Finally we return to Jesus' words to note that God had intended the Temple to be the place of prayer for all people. The story indicates, however, that prayer had not been possible for all people. The action in the story took place in the outer part of the Temple complex, the court of the Gentiles.[38] Thus the religious leaders had taken the only area allowed the Gentiles (and any Jew deemed too unclean to enter the sanctuary) for prayer and turned it into a place of commerce, exploitation, and violence. Though the Gentiles were supposed to be able to approach God through the Jewish faith, the religious leaders had made it impossible for them to pray to God in the Temple. Such action is another indication of how exclusive the religious leaders had made their religion. Jesus' words indicate again how inauthentic such exclusivity is before God.

These inauthentic responses to God's initiative to grant a place of prayer for all people indicate that, like the fig tree in leaf, the religious leaders were making a fair outward show in their worship in the Temple, but they had produced no fruit. The parables discourse (4:1–34) has already warned us to see through deceptive appearances, while the confrontation in 7:1–23 showed that the religious leaders had only an external spirituality. They had no righteousness in their hearts, no concern for justice for the oppressed or for the Gentiles. When Jesus indicated that their actions would doom them, they did not repent but plotted to destroy him instead. Truly their lives had produced no fruit whatsoever.

Immediately following the conclusion to the fig tree frame (vv. 20–21) is a discussion of faith and prayer (vv. 22–25) that gives us the authentic responses Jesus sought in this episode. A first glance may leave readers questioning what faith and prayer have to do with a withered fig tree. Remembering the double intercalation provides an answer: The prophecy of the destruction of the Temple (the "house of prayer") makes the prayer sayings relevant in this context.

Jesus' teaching on prayer contains three imperatives that indicate how he intended his followers to respond to what they had seen and heard from him. We begin with the second which is the present imperative "believe": "all things whatsoever you are praying and asking for, believe that you have received it, and it will be to you" (v. 24). The tenses of the verbs in this verse are significant. While followers continue praying and asking (present tense), they are commanded to believe that God's response, though it lies in the future ("it *will be* to you"), has already been given (past tense). Disciples' belief that they have already received that for which they are praying, though they do not have it yet, is the authentic response to God's gift of prayer.

The reason followers of Jesus are so to believe is found in the first imperative, which is in verse 22: "*have faith* in God." Jesus can command disciples to have faith, not because they are prone to be faithful (in fact, the disciples in Mark are prone to be exactly the opposite!), but because God is able to do the impossible, even to cast this mountain into the sea (v. 23a). The mountain-moving statement is another example of an *adynaton* like we saw in 9:23. It reinforces the declaration there that "all things are possible to the one who believes." As Mark reveals both here and in 9:14–29, he believes prayer is effective because Jesus showed God to be so powerful as to be able to do whatever followers ask in prayer.[39] The authentic response to such a God is to have faith and believe that one has received that for which one is praying.

We are given further understanding of faith in this text: Having faith in God means not doubting in one's heart (v. 23b). To doubt is to be inwardly divided or uncertain, or even to be hesitant.[40] According to this passage, such inward uncertainty or hesitancy about God's ability to do the impossible is precisely what may not be present in order for faith to be authentic and make a difference. Thus not doubting does not denote an especially strong faith but is what Jesus means by faith in these verses.[41]

Again, to avoid misunderstanding, we must note that just as "all things" in the phrase "all things are possible to the one who believes" (9:23) was not to be understood literally, so also "all things whatsoever" does not literally mean "all things" in 11:24. Careful scrutiny of Mark's Gospel has shown us that "all things" actually means all those things necessary for accomplishing God's will of setting people free for the life God intended for them. Close examination of this text confirms that understanding: Mark's Jesus did not speak of any mountain but of *this* mountain being cast into the sea (v. 23a). Many scholars believe he specifically meant the Temple Mount.[42] Thus his teaching is not that anything will happen through prayer (a mountain can be cast into the sea) but that evil (this mountain, meaning the Temple with all its oppressions) will be defeated through prayer to God whose power is greater than that of evil.

Now we are in position to grasp the significance of the second intercalation. The Temple had been the place for prayer so that prayers offered there were considered particularly effective. The destruction of the Temple (symbolized by the withered fig tree, v. 20) does not mean, however, that prayer is no longer available to God's people. The house of prayer is indeed judged and doomed, but Jesus claims it is replaced by persons of faith. For them prayer is still effective, even more so since the Temple actually hindered prayer. Clearly, then, ongoing faithful prayer to God who can move this mountain, even when all appearances are that this mountain (i.e., evil) is as immovable as ever, is an authentic response from disciples committed to God's will being done.

The final imperative of the section is in verse 25a: "when you stand praying, *forgive,* if you have anything against anyone." The reason for this command is "so that your father in heaven may forgive you your sins" (v. 25b). Three points are key. The first point is the sense of community that pervades the passage. Since sin in that world was a breach of interpersonal relations, forgiveness had the character of restoration to one's place within the community.[43] Furthermore, forgiving "anyone" constitutes disciples as an inclusive community open to "all nations" which fulfills the purpose that the cursed Temple had failed to achieve.[44] Clearly Mark believed God gave gifts for the benefit of all people. The second point is connected to the first: since Jesus has shown that God includes all people within God's *basileia* (7:1–30), we should not be surprised that disciples' forgiveness from God is tied to their forgiving others. How could disciples hope to be regarded by God as authentic if they refused to be like God in forgiving and including all within the community of faith? The third point has to do with the significance of Jesus referring to God as "father." The term certainly says nothing about God and gender, but it does evoke the parent-child relationship as a way of experiencing and claiming the relation to God who is thus portrayed as gracious and merciful.[45] Jesus' earlier statements indicate God's ability to overcome evil and accomplish God's will. Evoking the parent-child relationship points to God's willingness to do so and further encourages the response of faith from would-be disciples.

Summary of Mark 11:12–25

This complex miracle story tells of a God who has granted the privilege of and place for prayer to all people, though the "place" has now changed. Furthermore the story pictures God, working through Jesus, as taking the initiative to judge those who abuse this gift, and by implication any of God's good gifts, to serve evil purposes. Finally, God's power to effect the judgment God has made and to overcome evil is affirmed by this narrative.

The inauthentic responses to God's initiatives in this story begin with what was noted above—using God's gifts to serve evil purposes. In the particular incident here the religious and political elites were using God's gift of a house of prayer, the Temple (with its taxes, tithes, sacrifices, etc.), to advance their own interests to the disadvantage of the majority of the people. They were stealing the life of the people (12:44). They had also turned the outer court of the Temple into the place for gathering the results of their oppression and exploitation thus making prayer impossible for the Gentiles and those Jews who were allowed only into this part of the Temple. In so doing, the leaders advanced their exclusive view of their religion. Exclusiveness, exploitation, and oppression are inauthentic responses to God who embraces all people, but using the Temple—God's gift—to accomplish these things is so inauthentic that it prompts God to pass judgment on the Temple system and its leaders.

In addition, Jesus charged that the Temple had become a "den of robbers," indicating it was also a place of violence. With so much wealth changing hands in that area, the eruption of violence is not surprising. The leaders chose more violence when they responded to Jesus' pronouncement of judgment by plotting to kill him. Since Jesus had already condemned the exercise of power over others, and since he will not respond violently to the violence done to him, violence is shown clearly to be an inauthentic response to God. Furthermore, their plot to destroy his life contradicts the revelation of God as the God of Life and is as inauthentic here as it was in 3:6.

The religious leaders chose to seek his death out of envy. We saw in 7:22 that envy is an inauthentic response that makes one's heart unclean. Here we see how envy makes one unclean. It leads persons to violence and death and, thus, evil.

Though the religious leaders had the Temple as a house of prayer in which to meet with God, and though it apparently helped them appear religious (see, e.g., 12:38–40), when we look beneath the surface we see that they are like fig trees with leaves but no fruit. Here, as in 7:1–23, the externals are not enough to keep God from coming as Judge when there is no righteousness in the heart and no justice in the treatment of others. An externally beautiful but internally fruitless relationship with God and others is an inauthentic response to God.

The authentic responses Jesus seeks from followers include creation of a new "house of prayer" in the form of an inclusive community— one in which anyone can be forgiven anything—whose members have committed themselves to God's will rather than evil and continue to pray while believing (without doubting or hesitating, which would be inauthentic responses) that God has already answered their prayers. Obviously, then, forgiving others is an authentic response to God who forgives us. Just as obviously, using God's gift of prayer, and any of God's gifts, to benefit all is an authentic response to God. The members of this community have faith in God's power to do all things necessary for accomplishing God's will of setting people free for the life God intended for them. They believe God is able to cast this mountain (i.e., evil) into the sea. Furthermore, because they have experienced their relationship with God to be like that between a loving and merciful parent and a child, they believe that God will act to overcome evil. So, they continue to pray and have faith in God even when evil appears to be as unconquerable and immovable as a mountain. Again, what potential good news is given in Mark's teaching on prayer for persons struggling to be authentic disciples in a world as evil as this one!

Authentic Spirituality according to Mark

Now it remains for the insights gained in studying Mark to be brought together, synthesized, and analyzed. After all this study we are finally able to ask and answer: What is Mark's experience of God as shared in his Gospel? What is authentic spirituality in response to this experience? What is not authentic, according to Mark? Why is the conflict explicitly named in Mark the way of *the Lord* versus the way of *humanity?* How "appropriate-able" is Markan spirituality for twentieth-century, nearly twenty-first century Christians? These questions will guide the effort to present conclusions regarding Mark's spirituality.

Mark's Experience of God

In 1982 John R. Donahue examined what he called a "neglected factor" in Mark's theology, namely, Mark's understanding of God. He noted such things as Mark's affirmation of Jewish understandings of God (particularly monotheism), how he spoke of God usually as just "God" without attributions or ascriptions (only three exceptions in 9:37; 11:25; 12:27), and had only four references to God as "father" (quite a contrast to Matthew's forty-four references). Thus Donahue concluded that Mark's "sober and reserved" language about God communicates Mark's "reverential transcendence." Mark makes little attempt to explain or define God but affirms the dignity and sovereignty of God. Donahue claimed that Mark was more interested in Jesus speaking for God to teach people the gospel of God and call them to do the will of God.[1]

Certainly this study confirms Donahue's conclusions regarding Mark's view of God as far as they go. On the basis of Donahue's work,

95

and of other scholars as well, I have assumed the Jewish background of Mark's monotheism and Mark's view of God's dignity and found nothing to disconfirm these; study of the miracles affirmed Mark's belief in God's power and sovereignty; and I found no new ascriptions or attributes for God. But I believe our examination of key Markan passages enables us to fill out Mark's understanding of God much more fully. While Mark was not concerned to explain or define God, he was very much interested in what he believed God was doing in and through Jesus of Nazareth.

Mark's language about God is indeed "sober and reserved," bespeaking the mysteriousness and transcendence of God, but he also sensed that this transcendent God was one who had purposefully drawn near human beings in Jesus of Nazareth. We recall how the sense of the presence of God in the stilling of the storm and in the miracles that immediately follow that story was so strong that it elicited fear/numinous awe from disciples. But Mark also sensed that God had drawn near for a significant purpose, to do something new among human beings. We remember the subversiveness of Jesus' actions in the healing of a man's hand on the Sabbath and the declaration that true purity arose from a pure heart. He sought not merely to reform but to transform their way of relating to God. Thus we saw that when Mark's Jesus talked about new wine and new wineskins (2:22), he meant God was seeking to make life different from the way it was.

Mark further believed that God was one who revealed. Through Jesus the mystery of the *basileia* was given to those who would hear and see that it had drawn near and become reality in the mission of Jesus of Nazareth. Here is the new thing God is doing. There were neither trumpet blasts nor portents in the heavens. Jesus was only a peasant carpenter from a Galilean village. But Mark believed that God had inaugurated God's own *basileia* and made it experientially available through him. It is hidden from ordinary sight, hence, its mysteriousness. But those with "eyes to see" perceive its sure presence. Mark also believed that God revealed the cost of following Jesus and living within God's *basileia*. The costs could be persecution, suffering, even death. So, as encouragement to persevere through persecution, God revealed through Jesus the future fulfillment of the *basileia* that God is bringing about. The poetic, apocalyptic description of the return of the Son of man/New Human Being affirms that the *basileia* will come in power. The result of its coming in power will be vindication for the righteous ones who were not ashamed to follow Jesus.

Why was God's purpose so costly? Because, Mark believed, God is one who acts on behalf of all people. How God's inclusiveness stands out in the Second Gospel! We can recall how clearly Mark paints this portrait of God. First, Jesus teaches that God seeks those who are pure in heart, which means anyone—priests, Gentiles, women, peasants, lepers, children, anyone—can be welcomed into God's *basileia*. Second, Jesus insists that God has always given gifts for the benefit of all people. Thus, Holy Scripture is God's gift to enable love of God and neighbor, and the Temple was to have been a house of prayer for all nations. Mark believed that Jesus acted to restore these gifts to God's intent. Third, God acted through Jesus to ransom people from whatever binds them so that they are free to live as God intended in an inclusive community of service and solidarity with one another without structures of domination, subordination, exploitation, or oppression. Fourth, God's compassion and mercy toward all people are evident in Jesus' acceptance of the pained demands of the Syrophoenician woman, his reception of a child, the healing granted the hesitant and uncertain father of the demon-possessed boy, the promise of God's forgiveness, and by evoking the parent-child relationship between God and human beings. Additional study of Jesus' bringing practitioners of despised occupations (fishermen, 1:16–20; a tax collector, 2:13–14) and women (15:40–41) into his circle of disciples would strengthen this portrait of God's inclusiveness. Defenders of an exclusive religion which put themselves in places of honor and power, however, will oppose this view of God. Thus the costliness of Jesus' proclamation in Mark.

Finally, Mark experienced God as one who is powerful to achieve God's purpose. In Mark's Gospel, God is the Lord of history who is able to do all things necessary to accomplish God's will even in the face of great evil. Mark portrayed evil as a great dehumanizing power that leads to death. It is illustrated most obviously in the sea that threatened disciples and in the demons that possessed many people in the story. But we also saw it in the other things that suck life from people: rigid legalism that would have kept a man from being healed on the Sabbath; an external purity system that kept people far from God and outside the community of God's people based on their birth status; and the economic system of the Temple that hindered prayer and burdened the people with tithes, taxes, and tributes beyond their ability to pay. These expressions of evil are consistently presented in Mark as benefiting the few to the great disadvantage of the many. But just as consistently Mark shows Jesus asserting that God's power to bring life is always greater than the power of evil, that God is the Judge of evil. God's power is greater than a storm-tossed sea, a twelve-year illness, six thousand demons at once, an immovable mountain of evil (the Temple system), even greater than death (the demon-possessed boy and Jairus's daughter). Mark's God is the powerful God of Life.

Thus Mark affirmed that God, though indeed mysterious and transcendent, has drawn near through Jesus to establish the *basileia* of God that can give Life to all people. Though we cannot see how it is possible, though it is new and not what people expected, though we may have to wait until the future to experience the fullness of God's *basileia* ourselves, though evil throws death in the faces of those seeking to live in God's *basileia,* Mark believed that God had launched the *basileia* through the mission of Jesus, and God can and will bring it to its foreordained fulfillment.

Authentic Spirituality according to Mark

In response to this experience of what God is doing, Mark believed that authentic followers of Jesus should "see" (and "hear") that God's own *basileia* has drawn near and become experientially available through Jesus. This kind of "sight" stands out as particularly significant for Mark. Because things are not always what they seem to be, because appearances can be deceiving, because the *basileia* is a mystery, disciples must see "beneath the surface" to the truer story behind the story. Jesus of Nazareth may have appeared to be only a peasant carpenter from a village in Galilee, but those with eyes to see and ears to hear can perceive that God is at work through Jesus accomplishing God's purposes. No proofs are offered. God's work in Jesus is hidden so that only those with eyes to see can discern it.

This may be a good time to wonder, as many readers of Mark may have done over the centuries: Why is there so much mystery here? Why are there no proofs or signs or explanations? Frederick Buechner has given the best answer that I have read. Faith, he claimed, involves not being sure. It cannot be proved in the same way that "I can't prove the friendship of my friend. When I experience it, I don't need to prove it. When I don't experience it, no proof will do. . . . Almost nothing that makes any real difference can be proved,"[2] including God's presence. Mark would agree. Thus, there can be no proofs that God is at work in Jesus. There is only faith.

So, those who have eyes to see are called to respond with faith that God has indeed drawn near in Jesus, and has done so for their good. An awareness of the presence of the Holy always produces a sense of fearful awe, but Mark urged disciples to be drawn to God's presence, to trust in God as a merciful parent. Mark also urged followers to have faith that God will bring the *basileia* to its fulfillment because God is able to do all things necessary to accomplish God's will.

Moved by their sight and faith, authentic disciples respond by proclaiming and bearing witness to the gospel. Like Jesus, they do so not only with their words but also by their actions. In response to the revelation of God's inclusiveness and God's acting through Jesus to ransom people from whatever binds them, authentic followers form an inclusive community that practices the discipleship of equals. The key qualification for participation is a pure heart devoted to loving God and others. Everyone, therefore, can be welcomed. No "external" barriers will be used to exclude—not race, class, ethnicity, gender, age, or physical condition. Furthermore, within the community of authentic followers there will be no barriers to living life as God intended—no structures of domination, subordination, exploitation, or oppression. Instead there is solidarity among them as disciples serve each other, even and especially the least ones, forgive each other, and have compassion for each other. They choose to do good and save life and are willing to take courageous, faithful action on behalf of others who are hurting. They receive God's good gifts as God intended—to benefit all of them. Devotion and obedience to Holy Scripture, for example, leads them to greater love of God and others, while the inclusive community becomes the new "house of prayer for all nations" in which authentic disciples open themselves to God's power through ongoing, faithful prayer. This community is the *basileia* of God made experientially available. It is indeed new wine. Instead of the same old game with merely a different set of players, Mark believed that God called authentic followers of Jesus to a whole new way of living and being God's people in the world.

Interestingly, Mark also shows that creating this community is not easy. In the story of the Syrophoenician woman, a very human Jesus struggled with the radical inclusiveness of God. Mark himself is not entirely consistent in recounting the inclusiveness of Jesus' movement. He tells readers that women were always part of the group of disciples only near the end of his story (15:40–41). His references to the Twelve, particularly Peter, James, and John, make readers likely to conclude that "disciples" refers to an all-male group (which would not be very inclusive) until Mark tells us otherwise at the end. Clearly, achieving the community that Mark believed God intended for us requires disciples to have pure hearts open to new ways of thinking about and relating to one another.

Because this new way of living and being God's people threatens the old ways, it often arouses opposition. Those who benefit from the world as is often are not interested in having that world subverted. Jesus' call to disciples to be alert and not caught off guard by his return works equally well as a call not to be caught off guard by persecution and suffering for the gospel. In such circumstances authentic disciples do not bend all their energies toward preserving their lives in this world but deny themselves by accepting the consequences of proclaiming the gospel (Jesus called this "taking up the cross") and persevering in their faith despite persecution. Furthermore, they trust the Holy Spirit to enable them to continue bearing witness to the gospel even as they are being persecuted. According to Mark, therefore, being an authentic disciple of Christ requires a radical commitment of one's whole heart to this new way of living and being the people of God, for it is a costly spirituality.

Followers can draw courage to make such a radical commitment from their faith that Jesus spoke the truth when he portrayed God as the Lord of history and the God of Life. Authentic disciples may risk losing their lives in this world because they believe they will have Life in God when the *basileia* comes in power, evil is finally overcome, and the righteous ones are gathered together to be with the risen and glorified Christ. They resist temptations to yield to despair even when life is chaotic and evil appears to be winning because of this faith in God. This moment is an appropriate one to reflect on the example of Jesus. He persisted in pursuing God's will despite persecution and lost his life. In the stark portrayal of the crucifixion in Mark, evil appears to have defeated Jesus. But appearances are often deceiving! Mark affirms that God was still at work and resurrected Christ (16:6), though he does not narrate any resurrection appearances of Jesus.[3] Instead Mark tells disciples that they will see Jesus "going before them" if they have faith to follow him (16:7). Faith and sight again! These alone (no proofs), Mark's narrative suggests, lead followers to Life in God.

From the perspective of Life in God, welcoming others into the community and practicing the discipleship of equals in this world matters greatly. These actions have ultimate consequences. A sense of eschatological urgency can fuel the commitment of authentic followers. But this urgency is not to be a blind urgency that focuses so much on the end that it forgets what should be done now. Authentic disciples must not be deceived by messianic pretenders, by those doing signs and wonders, or by those who claim to use current events—war, earthquakes, famine—to calculate the when of the end. Instead they continue their proclamation of God's gospel, even during persecution, without giving in to fear because they trust in God's ultimate fulfillment of the *basileia* in God's own timing (only God knows the hour). They are able to "see" that God is at work through the Spirit who is with them and thus maintain their hopeful anticipation of God's defeat of evil and vindication of all that is good and gives Life so that they persevere to the end. Thus we come at the end of the description of authentic Markan spirituality to what has colored the description throughout: "seeing" and the deep faith that is so closely related to it.

Inauthentic Spirituality according to Mark

Mark also provides a significant presentation of the types of responses to God he felt authentic disciples must not make. He uses the responses of two different groups to portray what he considers to be inauthentic spirituality. There are those, like the first seed in the parable of the sower, who never hear Jesus' word but choose evil from the outset. The religious leaders, with assistance from the Herodians and Romans, in Mark's story comprise this group. Then there are those, like the second and third seed in the parable, who hear Jesus' word, who appear to have joined the community of Jesus' followers, but whose responses are nonetheless judged as inauthentic. The disciples, perhaps surprisingly, often reflect these responses. The responses of the two groups, while not identical, are remarkably similar in places. It may be significant for Mark that both groups, even those who choose evil from the outset, appear to be very religious.

A whole set of inauthentic responses that stand out as particularly significant fall into a category that could be named "Focus on One's Own or One's Group's Interests."[4] The religious leaders used God's gifts, which were intended to benefit all people, for their own advantage and the disadvantage of others. Their enforcement of a purity code based on externals and surfaces created an exclusive religion with themselves in the central, privileged place. They insisted on literal adherence to scripture when it served their interests to do so (e.g., keeping food laws). But they were willing to promote their human traditions at the expense of scripture when doing so worked to their advantage. Their rigidly legalistic approach to either scripture or human tradition produced observable ways to measure their holiness—they fasted, did ritual washings, refused to eat with tax collectors and sinners, observed the Sabbath strictly, and so forth. These activities enabled them to elevate themselves further over the masses. Finally, they used the Temple to promote both their central place and their wealth while keeping the "rabble" far from the Holy of Holies where God was considered to reside.

The religious leaders responded inauthentically in other ways. Their abuse of the Temple also reveals their lust for wealth and other things (power, honor, privilege) which, as the sower parable showed, resulted in fruitlessness (no justice or righteousness). They were envious of Jesus, fearful that the crowds might follow his leadership rather than theirs. They exercised "power over" others to keep their privileged place. They dominated and exploited the masses through their teaching and through the redistribution system of the Temple to the point of robbing the life from many; and they used violence when necessary in the Temple and in dealing with the threat Jesus presented. Thus they displayed no respect for life and often caused death, either literally or figuratively, which is Mark's understanding of evil. The results of their focus on themselves are hard, compassionless hearts not the least bit concerned for loving God and others, willing to do nothing when someone is in need to preserve their tradition, willing to do whatever is necessary to maintain their place at the top of their world.

Some of those who heard Jesus' word were also guilty of concentrating on themselves. The disciples left everything to follow Jesus (10:29), but they too were concerned with their "place."[5] They argued over who was the greatest among them, showing themselves to be envious of one another and desirous of the places of honor in God's *basileia*. They showed little interest in the least ones and tried to keep children away from Jesus. Then, when persecution arose, they were more interested in preserving their own lives than in their commitment to the Way of the Lord: Peter denied Jesus (14:66–72) after the other disciples had fled (14:50). Their actions suggest they were concerned for what they could gain for themselves by joining Jesus with little consideration for what the cost might be.

Perhaps as a consequence of their focus on themselves, inauthentic followers of Jesus, according to Mark, cannot "see" God's revelation. Those who choose evil never even attempt to see or hear or understand what God is doing through Jesus. But even some of those who heard Jesus' word could not "see." The disciples apparently could not see that God was doing something new, that the *basileia* meant an inclusive community that practices the discipleship of equals. Like many persons who have suffered under an oppressive religious-political-economic system, the disciples only want to change those who run the show. They do not see that the hierarchical system operative in their world (the few on top; the others on bottom) is inherently oppressive so that merely changing those at the top would actually change nothing. Furthermore, they could not see that suffering for the gospel is an inevitable result of doing God's will (precisely because it is new and subverts the world). Instead, they are caught off guard and not alert to the situation they face (remember the sleep of Peter, James, and John in Gethsemane). Also, they appear to be easily deceived. For example, they comment on the beauty of the Temple, apparently unable to see its fruitlessness. Jesus' warnings in 8:15 ("Look, see the yeast of the Pharisees and the yeast of Herod") and 12:38–40 ("see" the religious leaders who love to wear long robes and have the best seats in the synagogues but "devour widows' houses and for a pretense make long prayers") hint at disciples' inability to see beneath the surface of an outward show of religion. And Jesus feels the need to warn them against being deceived by messianic pretenders, those doing signs and wonders, and those who claim to have calculated the time of the end. Though Mark's Jesus admonishes them repeatedly, inauthentic disciples do not "hear" his call to "see."

As authentic sight and deep faith were closely connected, so an inability to see is also linked to a shallow, rootless faith that does not persevere to the end. Falling away before persecution (as the disciples did) suggests a lack of faith in Jesus' teaching that God will stand with disciples against evil, that the Spirit will be present to enable them to bear witness, that God's power is greater than that of evil and thus God can do all things necessary to accomplish God's will, and that God as Lord of history will ultimately vindicate unjust suffering. Lack of faith leads to a lack of prayer and perhaps to efforts to rely on one's own power instead. It also leads, when confronted by the power of evil, to doubt, uncertainty, hesitancy, and even despair.

Both the religious leaders and the disciples exhibit a lack of openness to the new thing God is doing. Indeed the religious leaders are adamantly opposed to anything new, while the disciples cannot see that God is doing far more than merely reforming the old ways. Closely related is the response of dread (or literal fear) of and turning away from God's near presence, perhaps due to awareness that God may well demand change (repentance).

Readers of Mark's Gospel are probably not surprised at the inauthenticity of the responses of the religious leaders who are opposed to Jesus from the beginning. They may not be surprised at the authentic responses that arise from so many of the "minor" characters in Mark's story: for example, the Syrophoenician woman who grasps God's radical inclusiveness, the Gerasene demoniac and the hemorrhaging woman whose fear/awe draws them to God's presence, and the anointing woman and Bartimaeus who "see" what Jesus' destiny must be. But readers may well be surprised at Mark's portrayal of the disciples as those who sometimes respond authentically to Jesus but more often do not. Perhaps Mark felt the disciples in his story reflected the disciples in his community. Thus, just as Jesus taught, rebuked, corrected, and challenged disciples in the story to respond authentically to God, so Mark wrote his Gospel to teach, rebuke, correct, and challenge disciples in his community to respond in the same way.[6] He desired his community members to leave inauthentic responses behind and become wholly authentic followers of Christ. His Gospel still challenges readers to this growth.

The Way of the Lord
versus the Way of Humanity

We are now able to "see" a number of reasons that Mark's narrative suggests naming the conflict at the heart of his story "The Way of the Lord versus the Way of Humanity" instead of something like "God versus Satan," as a number of readers might have expected. Remember how those persons making inauthentic responses to God's initiatives focused on themselves and/or their group's interests. They can see only "on the surface," only with human eyes. Consequently, they are not open to change or newness but are interested instead in figuring out how to make it in the only reality they see—like the disciples who wished to replace the first ones and great ones with themselves instead of seeing a new community of service and solidarity without structures of domination. They wish to "gain the whole world." They signal no concern for Life in God. In other words, these persons are focused on the here and now, on what people are doing, and on how they can best benefit from what humans have created. Thus it appears that Mark has aptly suggested through his narrative that the name for inauthentic spirituality be "the Way of Humanity."

Some qualifying remarks are in order, however. First, the name "Way of Humanity" does not mean that Mark has a negative view of human beings as dirty rotten scoundrels, corrupt to the core, who deserve to go straight to hell. On the contrary, the God in Mark's story is greatly interested in and shows compassion for all human beings. Indeed, loving others ranks alongside loving God as the greatest commandments. The problem with followers of the Way of Humanity is that they focus on too few human beings—themselves and their group. Second, there is no doubt that followers of the Way of Humanity serve the purposes of Satan. Their focus on themselves leads them to harm and devalue others and to rob the life from many, which is exactly what the power of evil causes in Mark's story. Still, the narrative suggests the name "Way of Humanity." I think that in doing so, Mark shows how subtle and insidious the power of evil is. Both the religious leaders and the disciples appear to be religious and would claim to be serving God. They do not, or will not, see that they are really serving themselves and thus succeed in serving only evil.

Appropriating Mark's Spirituality Today

The final question to consider is, Can a spirituality forged in the second half of the first century nurture an authentic spirituality for Christians who live more than nineteen hundred years later?

We should acknowledge that Mark does not offer a complete spirituality for disciples either in his day or in ours. For example, he has only limited discussions of the appropriate use of material possessions, prayer (he does not even have the Lord's Prayer), and the role of the Spirit in the lives of disciples (nothing like Paul's lists of spiritual gifts). Nothing in his story is related to such concerns as discovering one's vocation, how community members should be accountable to one another, or what makes for a healthy, sacred expression of one's sexuality. Thus we need to study the whole New Testament, and indeed all of Christian tradition, to enable us to become wholly authentic followers of Christ.

But Mark, as part of the New Testament and also as part of the tradition, offers a consistent presentation of spirituality with potentially profound insights to offer Christians from what is present in its pages.

We should no longer neglect Mark (as I sense has been done) when we turn to the New Testament to nurture our spirituality.

We can begin mining Mark's gems[7] by noting the continuing relevance of his exhortation through narrative not to use God's gifts to advance personal interests/ In a short time we could make a long list of ways religious leaders have abused their positions in the church to gain power and wealth at others' expense. As a North American Protestant, I am particularly horrified by the use of the Bible to justify any number of great evils in Western history. Slavery, anti-Semitism (including Hitler's "final solution"), the efforts of white missionaries to destroy the cultures of the people they went to evangelize, "just" wars, and apartheid in South Africa are ugly examples of efforts to advance the power and wealth of mainly white Americans and Europeans in which the Bible played significant roles. As a Protestant woman, I am particularly affected by ways the Bible has been used to subjugate women and keep men in positions of power and authority in both church and society. Woman's inferior status, the insistence for many years that marriage and motherhood were a woman's only destiny, the call to women to be submissive even to indifferent or abusive husbands, encouragement to battered wives to stay with their husbands (for a variety of reasons: divorce is a sin, this is the "cross" you must bear, suffer silently and continue to love him in order to win him to the Lord, and so on), praising women's self-negation as a virtue,[8] and the position that a woman cannot be called to ministry are some of the oppressions women have faced that have been drawn from the Bible and preached resolutely from many pulpits.

Never mind that women could draw on stories of Jesus' treatment of women and other biblical texts to make exactly the opposite case. Never mind that Jesus used the Bible to promote love of God and all people. Never mind the great suffering that has been aided and abetted by these uses of the Bible. It seems to me that too many ministers in Europe and the United States have been among those who apparently liked sitting atop the "world as is," wanted change no more than the religious leaders of Jesus' day, and used the Bible to justify their positions. Let us remember, however, that nothing made Mark's Jesus angrier than the use of God's good gifts to advance the interests of the few to the detriment of the many/ Church history with its catalog of abuses defended by means of the Bible affirms his anger as absolutely justified. We must know that such a response to God's gifts is as inauthentic as ever.

There is a simple segue from discussion of the abuse of God's gifts for personal gain to consideration of Mark's call to form an inclusive community that practices the discipleship of equals, Mark regarded such a community as an authentic response to the revelation of God's inclusiveness and compassion for all people. This call was new wine that needed new wineskins in the days of Jesus and Mark. How sad that it is still new wine today! Early in its history the church moved toward hierarchy and exclusivism and, with precious few exceptions, has remained so until today.[9] How many different ways is the church practicing an external purity today? In my opinion, however, there is good news. In the last three decades prophetic voices have been heard more clearly than ever calling the church to renew its community practices according to the teachings of Jesus, including his teachings in Mark. Latin American liberation theologians have decried the class structures operative in the church which prevent it from being an advocate for the poor and suffering ones in Central and South America. Black theologians challenge white churches to admit and repent of their racism and embrace the contributions of Africans and African Americans to our understanding of what it means to be Christian. Feminist theologians seek to clear away the last stumbling block to the practice of the discipleship of equals by exposing the consequences and challenging the power of a few men over women and marginalized men. Feminists in particular have reminded Christians that changing the people who run the church is not enough when the hierarchical structures of the church are inherently oppressive. These voices tell us we still need to drink from the new wine of Mark's vision of an inclusive community of equals if we would reflect the God of the Second Gospel and live within the *basileia* God launched through Jesus.

In this context we should recall Mark's antiviolent position. Violence, as has been noted, is a particularly ugly expression of "power over" another. In Mark's story violence leads to Jesus' death and serves the purposes of evil, while Jesus steadfastly refuses to engage in violence to save himself. The inauthenticity of violence as a response to God who embraces and has compassion for all people could hardly be clearer. Yet the church's history is awfully bloody. Think of the Crusades, the Inquisitions, the witch trials, Northern Ireland, and so on. During the spring that I worked on this book a Lutheran woman in Pontotoc, Mississippi, objected to the prayers being said over the intercoms at her children's schools. As ministers led rallies against her, rocks were thrown through her windows, and she and her children were threatened by people who insisted that God be kept in the schools. What is wrong with this picture? Similarly, some antiabortion Christians in this country participate in threatening and harassing clinic staffers, doctors, and even doctors' families. While the actual murders of doctors was doubtlessly done by fringe members, other Christians in the movement have been unwilling to see the evil environment their violent rhetoric has created and reluctant to repudiate the violence.

All the above circumstances and activities suggest that Mark's call to followers of Jesus to *see* is as needed as ever. Since God revealed the mystery of the *basileia* to followers, Mark believed authentic disciples would understand it, would see beneath surface appearances to the truer story behind the story. This aspect of authentic spirituality seems particularly appropriate for Christians in a society like ours that too often values style over substance and is too often swayed by thirty-second sound bites. Authentic Christians should be able to see, for example, through outward shows of religion. Supporting school prayer is considered a public assertion that one is religious. But I wonder if it enables persons to have pure hearts that love God and others. In other words, what kind of fruit does it bear? Furthermore, it seems to me to be easier to rally for prayer in school than to respect, listen to, and include people who view circumstances differently. But Mark warns us away from an easy spirituality. Authentic Christians should also be able to see whether their community of faith is striving to welcome everyone into God's *basileia* and practicing the discipleship of equals or if ego and power interests are still at work.

Consider the following dialogue drawn from a recent popular mystery novel:

> "Plus," he added, "any form of organized belief in God is an excuse for one person to say to another, 'Believe as I do or you'll go to hell, or I'll burn you at the stake, or I'll kill you and the horse you rode in on *and* everyone else who thinks like you.'"
>
> Deep down, Kate felt it had been worth driving 269 miles just to hear those words. "So it's about power?"
>
> "The most powerful and destructive of all the aphrodisiacs."[10]

Many Christians, myself included, would respond to such statements by claiming it is not belief in God but persons who are using belief in God to gain power that leads to such behavior. While we may have a point, it is still true that too often Christians have not seen such persons for what they are and have not resisted what they are doing. Instead, if a person is charismatic, looks right, and sounds good (uses the right words and can quote scripture), many Christians are ready to follow blindly without examining the fruits the person is bearing/ In other words, I fear the church has earned the scorn of the above novelist and others like her. It is past time that we see that Mark does not call for blind faith. Instead, Mark calls for deeply insightful faith.

Because I am a minister, I feel I should point out that all of the above comments place a special responsibility on ministers to *see* ourselves, to know what we are about, to examine the fruits of our lives and our ministries. Invoking God's name is a powerful tool for persuading people to feel, think, and do various things. It seems to me that invoking it for personal gain is an aspect of what is meant by taking God's name in vain. Both Mark and Moses would say to us, "Thou shalt not!" We ministers should constantly ask ourselves and each other if we are responding to God's initiatives like the religious leaders in Mark's story, like the disciples, or like the Syrophoenician woman.

There is one other way that Mark calls Christians to *see* that is particularly appropriate for Christians today. Jesus in Mark warns disciples to see and not be deceived by messianic pretenders or by those calculating the time of the end. As we approach the year 2000 we can expect, I believe, a plethora of predictions from persons claiming to speak uniquely for God. There will doubtlessly be books, TV shows, radio programs, sermons from pulpits, and Sunday school lessons devoted to calculating the when of the end. But Mark would say to us, *"See! Keep alert! Don't be deceived! No one knows except God!"*

In addition to the gems just examined, we should note that Mark has significant teaching on prayer to share with those who have a growing interest in spirituality. There is not much on prayer in Mark, but what is there is engaging. The healing of the demon-possessed boy and the fig tree/Temple intercalation proclaim God's power to do all things necessary to accomplish God's purposes. We should remember how Mark's Gospel qualified "all things are possible" and "whatever you ask for in prayer." Both stories teach us that through prayer we open ourselves to the power of God to overcome even a "mountainous" evil. It may be no coincidence that the three times Mark records Jesus praying are all at night; we know that darkness is a common symbol for evil (see 1:35; 6:45–48; 14:17, 32–42). The fig tree story in particular suggests that God always intended for persons to have access to

God through prayer and that ongoing prayer is a sign of faith in God. Conversely, lack of prayer would signal lack of faith. Though Mark does not answer all our questions about prayer (How should we pray? If we fail to pray, then does God not act against evil?), the Second Gospel teaches that authentic prayer is faithful and continuous, effective against evil and for God's purposes, and not selfish but focused on accomplishing God's will.

The final Markan gem to be appraised is his insistence that authentic disciples will commit themselves radically to the gospel even to the point of losing their lives for Jesus' sake. In the hands of hierarchical leaders in the history of the church Jesus' call in Mark to deny self, take up the cross, and lose one's life in order to gain it has been used to promote self-sacrifice, passive acceptance of suffering (any suffering), humility, meekness, and more. So slaves, oppressed workers, marginalized peoples, middle-class women in bad marriages, have been told to accept their lot in life, suffer in silence, and "just trust God" to make it all better "by and by." No wonder Karl Marx responded with his famous description of religion as "the opiate of the people." The irony is that Mark's Jesus calls for exactly the opposite response from authentic disciples! Because of their faith in God as Lord of history who has made the *basileia* experientially available now and is bringing it to its divinely ordained fulfillment, authentic disciples do not passively accept their lot in life. Instead, they deny themselves and take up the cross in order to change the world in favor of an inclusive community of God's people that practices the discipleship of equals. In other words, they risk their lives to make possible now what God will fulfill in God's future.

Since those who profit from the world as is usually do not want change, Mark believed the suffering of authentic disciples was inevitable. A number of scholars contend that Mark's pessimism is overstated and can lead to a glorification of suffering that is unwise and unhealthy. They remind us that change can come about more peacefully. Though we can and have named Christians who have lost their lives for the gospel (Bonhoeffer, King, Romero, etc.), most Christians today will probably not have to put their lives on the line for their faith.

While Mark may have overstated his case,[11] many of us have witnessed good reasons for disciples to *see* the costs of following Christ. African-American Christians in the civil rights movement faced rocks, fire hoses, billy clubs, and worse as they sought equality. Dr. King was not, unfortunately, the only one who died. The few white Christians who joined them suffered as well. My ethics professor in seminary, Dr. Henlee Barnett, had to leave Birmingham, Alabama, after marching with Dr. King. Later he joined the faculty at Southern Baptist Theological Seminary where, in 1962, Dr. King was invited to speak in chapel over the protests of white church members. His appearance cost the seminary $250,000 in contributions withheld.[12]

Other examples of the costs of being an authentic disciple as Mark envisioned it include the silencing of Latin American liberation theologians by the Roman Catholic Church during the 1980s. Dr. Elisabeth Schüssler Fiorenza, the foremost theorist of a liberating interpretation of scripture for women and a Roman Catholic, has not taught full-time in a Roman Catholic school since the mid-1970s because of her advocacy of women's rights and roles in the church and beyond.[13] Although none were actually harmed, the members of the inclusive language lectionary committee and their families faced death threats as the lectionaries were published in 1983, 1984, and 1985; Dr. Susan Brooks Thistlethwaite told of threats made against her and her family in a presentation at the American Academy of Religion (AAR) Annual Meeting in Philadelphia on November 21, 1995; New Testament scholar Thomas Hoyt confirmed that he had similar experiences in a conversation on December 11, 1995. Dr. Molly Marshall was forced to resign from the faculty at Southern Baptist Theological Seminary in 1994 for supporting women in ministry and the discipleship of equals in church and theology. A Presbyterian minister couple in Pontotoc, Mississippi, who supported women in ministry and justice for the poor had to leave their church in the spring of 1995. Their pastoral care for the woman who objected to prayer in the schools was the proverbial last straw for their church. These are a few of the circumstances of "suffering" with which I am familiar. Readers may well be able to add to this list.

Why and how would persons persist in the face of persecutions like those named above, even to the point at times of risking their lives? Mark gives a twofold answer to that question. First, in the words of the sower parable, authentic disciples have *heard* the word of God and accepted it so that it bears much fruit. They have deep roots of faith. They have *seen* Jesus' word as God's truth. They have experienced the presence of the *basileia* now in Jesus. They will *not* turn away from it. Second, according to the message of the seed parable, authentic disciples anticipate with great hope that God is bringing about the fulfillment of God's word as God has promised to do. They believe in God's

future, in *life* in God, that the *basileia* is coming in power. So their following Jesus "on the Way" is not in vain, even if they see little fulfillment during their lifetimes, for they have joined themselves to both
the present and the future of God.

Now we must ask a last question: Is this first-century vision of the
present and future of God viable at the end of the twentieth-century?
Here is where the "rubber meets the road" for many people. Some
Christians have no trouble answering this question with a definite yes.
But other people, Christians and non-Christians alike, think of the
nineteen hundred plus years that have passed since Mark wrote, all the
changes that have occurred both in the way we live and in the way we
think, the continuing (and increasing?) presence of evil, and how little the church seems to have improved in all those years, and wonder
if they can believe that God is the Lord of history who is bringing creation to a just fulfillment. I will not presume to be able to answer that
question definitively in these pages. But as a means of offering help to
those wrestling with Mark's experience of God and their own sense of
faith and history, I point out the following observations of thoughtful,
contemporary theologians regarding the future. German Protestant
theologian Jürgen Moltmann believes that God's essential nature is the
future. Thus the resurrection of Jesus anticipates a new eschatological
future for all creation which does not yet exist in all its fullness. God
calls persons, as we live in the time of the "not yet," to an active life
of hope made possible by God's promises.[14] Catholic theologian Johann Baptist Metz claims that what motivates hope is the free future
of God: "This is an understanding of history and the future in which
the future becomes visible . . . as forbearance, forgiveness, and recon-
ciliation."[15] Liberationist and feminist theologian Dorothee Soëlle insists that a church which has no sense of the future, which is stuck in
the "now already" will revolve around itself and no longer expect
God. This self-sufficiency "contradicts the message of Jesus, which
points the disciples towards a greater expectation of festival, of joy, of
laughter for all." Indeed, she says, the church should be "the expression of a waiting for God, a longing for the heavenly Jerusalem."[16]

So, after reflection on Holy Scripture, the history of the church,
and their own contemporary situation, these theologians and others
like them find that hope for the future continues to be an integral part
of their faith in God. Perhaps no one in our time has expressed this
hope more concretely, poignantly, or poetically than Martin Luther
King Jr. on the night before he was killed:

We've got some difficult days ahead. But it really doesn't matter with me now, because I've been to the mountaintop. And I don't mind. Like anybody, I would like to live a long life. . . . But I'm not concerned about that now. I just want to do God's will. And He's allowed me to go up to the mountain. And I've looked over. And I've seen the promised land. I may not get there with you. But I want you to know tonight that we as a people will get to the promised land. And I'm happy tonight, I'm not worried about anything. I'm not fearing any man. Mine eyes have seen the glory of the coming of the Lord.[17]

Perhaps Dr. King's poetry is not so different from Mark's: "Then they will see the Son of man/New Human Being coming in clouds with great power and glory. Then he will send out the angels and gather his elect from the four winds, from the ends of earth to the ends of heaven" (13:26–27). If so, then perhaps Mark's vision of the present and future of God is viable at the end of the twentieth century. Perhaps it is indeed possible for contemporary Christians who desire to be authentic followers of Jesus to be nurtured by Mark's spirituality and to heed Mark's invitation to see and believe and proclaim and serve and persist and hope along the Way of the Lord.

Notes

Notes to Introduction

1. Stephen C. Barton, *The Spirituality of the Gospels* (Peabody, Mass.: Hendrickson Publishers, 1992), 3, offers this description of the New Testament Gospels: "They are 'faith documents' from start to finish—written expressions of profound encounters with the divine, intended to mediate those experiences to others as the basis for faith, repentance and new life." Though I do not use his words, my view of the New Testament is in agreement with his.

2. I am sure there are Christians whose favorite book, even before taking a seminary class, is Mark, but I have not met them. My experience suggests to me that such Christians are few.

3. Indeed, the identity of this author remains one of the unsolved mysteries of Markan studies. For the sake of convenience I will simply refer to the author as "Mark" without intending to identify her or him with any specific person. Furthermore, I will use the masculine pronoun for this author when a pronoun is necessary. Though suggestions by some scholars that the author may have been a woman interest me, the odds favor his having been male. But one can hope.

4. Bonnie Thurston, *Spiritual Life in the Early Church* (Minneapolis: Fortress Press, 1993), ix, has this comment on the work of biblical scholars: "In recent years there has been a great hunger in the churches for a more profound spiritual life. Either because we have lost touch with our brothers and sisters in the pews or because we somehow view the field of spirituality as at best suspect and at worst beneath our notice, we in the academy have done little to feed that hunger."

5. Sandra M. Schneiders, "The Johannine Resurrection Narratives: An Exegetical and Theological Study of John 20 as a Synthesis of Johannine Spirituality," vol. 1 (Ph.D. diss., Pontificia Universitas Gregoriana, 1975), xxv–xxvi.

6. Sharyn E. Dowd, "New Testament Theology and the Spirituality of Early Christianity: Relationships and Implications," *Lexington Theological Quarterly* 24 (1989): 70.

7. Carolyn Osiek, "Editor's Preface," in Karen A. Barta, *The Gospel of*

Mark, Message of Biblical Spirituality, vol. 9 (Wilmington, Del.: Michael Glazier, 1988), 9.

8. Barton, *Spirituality of the Gospels,* 2.
9. Louis Bouyer, *The Spirituality of the New Testament and the Fathers,* A History of Christian Spirituality, vol. 1, trans. Mary P. Ryan (1960; reprint Minneapolis: Winston Press, 1963), 90.
10. Dowd, "New Testament Theology," 77–78.
11. Edward Kinerk, "Toward a Method for the Study of Spirituality," *Review for Religious* 40 (1981): 3, 5; Anne E. Carr, *Transforming Grace: Christian Tradition and Women's Experience* (San Francisco: Harper & Row, 1988), 201–2.
12. Kinerk, "Toward a Method," 6.
13. Jon Alexander claimed that recently Roman Catholic writers have often employed "spirituality" in an experiential sense in "What Do Recent Writers Mean by Spirituality?" *Spirituality Today* 32 (1980): 251. Roman Catholic writers are not alone. Southern Baptist Loyd Allen maintained that at the core of all approaches to spirituality "lies the reality of humanity's meeting with the divine," in "Spirituality Among Southern Baptist Clergy as Reflected in Selected Autobiographies" (Ph.D. diss., The Southern Baptist Theological Seminary, 1984), 16.
14. Kinerk, "Toward a Method," 6.
15. Adolf Deissmann, *Paul: A Study in Social and Religious History,* 2d ed., trans. William E. Wilson (1927; reprint Gloucester, Mass.: Peter Smith, 1972), 150. Deissmann actually used the phrase "reacting mysticism" instead of "reacting spirituality," but since he proposed to give the name "*Mystik* to every religious tendency that discovers the way to God direct through inner experience" (149), I believe I am correct in understanding what he means by mysticism to be very close to what I mean by spirituality.
16. Denise Lardner Carmody, *Seizing the Apple: A Feminist Spirituality of Personal Growth* (New York: Crossroad, 1984), 41.
17. Carr, *Transforming Grace,* 201–2; Kinerk, "Toward a Method," 12–13; Sandra M. Schneiders, *Women and the Word: The Gender of God in the New Testament and the Spirituality of Women* (New York: Paulist Press, 1986), 15–19.

Notes to Chapter 1

1. Thomas H. Tobin, *The Spirituality of Paul,* The Message of Biblical Spirituality Series, vol. 12 (Wilmington, Del.: Michael Glazier, 1987), 13.
2. John J. Collins, "The Rediscovery of Biblical Narrative," *Chicago Studies* 21 (1982): 54–56.
3. I am drawing on the work of Sandra M. Schneiders, *The Revelatory Text: Interpreting the New Testament as Sacred Scripture* (San Francisco: Harper, 1991), in which she calls for attention to be paid to the world of the text and also to the world in front of the text, which is those of us who are reading the text. She claims that until we respond to what

the text offers us, the interpretation of the text isn't complete. See esp. 153–54, 167–69.

4. Jack Dean Kingsbury, *The Christology of Mark's Gospel* (Philadelphia: Fortress Press, 1983), 47–48; Norman R. Petersen, "'Point of View' in Mark's Narrative," *Semeia* 12 (1978): 107.

5. Edward Kinerk, "Toward a Method for the Study of Spirituality," *Review for Religious* 40 (1981): 8.

6. It is my decision to translate the recurring Greek word *anthropos* in these verses as "human" or "humanity" since the word is obviously referring to the whole human race and not just the male half of it.

7. Petersen, "Point of View," 108.

8. John R. Donahue, "A Neglected Factor in the Theology of Mark," *Journal of Biblical Literature* 101 (1982): 566, 569.

9. Kinerk, "Toward a Method," 10.

Notes to Chapter 2

1. G. H. Boobyer, "The Redaction of Mark IV. 1–34," *New Testament Studies* 8 (1962): 61–64; Christopher D. Marshall, *Faith as a Theme in Mark's Narrative* (Cambridge: Cambridge University Press, 1989), 60.

2. Aloysius Ambrozic, *The Hidden Kingdom: A Redactional-Critical Study of the References to the Kingdom of God in Mark's Gospel,* Catholic Biblical Quarterly Monograph Series 2 (Washington, D.C.: Catholic Biblical Association of America, 1972), 84.

3. C. H. Dodd, *The Parables of the Kingdom,* 3d ed. (London: Nisbet & Co., 1935), 5.

4. John R. Donahue, *The Gospel in Parable: Metaphor, Narrative, and Theology in the Synoptic Gospels* (Philadelphia: Fortress Press, 1988), 9.

5. Werner H. Kelber, *The Oral and the Written Gospel* (Philadelphia: Fortress Press, 1983), 60–64, 73.

6. Marcus J. Borg, *Jesus: A New Vision* (New York: Harper & Row, 1987), 26–27. Borg gives a thorough discussion of this worldview in the Bible, 27–34.

7. Donahue, *Gospel in Parable,* 9–11.

8. James G. Williams, *Gospel against Parable: Mark's Language of Mystery* (Sheffield: JSOT Press, 1985), 79.

9. Those interested in the arguments in favor of Mark's having composed this discourse from various Jesus sayings should see the following sources: Hugh Anderson, *The Gospel of Mark,* New Century Bible Commentary (Grand Rapids: Wm. B. Eerdmans Publishing Co., 1976), 127–30, 132–33, 135, 136, 138–40; Eduard Schweizer, *The Good News according to Mark,* trans. Donald H. Madvig (Atlanta: John Knox Press, 1970), 89–90, 92–93, 96, 99, 103, 105–6; C. E. B. Cranfield, "St. Mark 4:1–34," part 2, *Scottish Journal of Theology* 5 (1952): 49–66. The various sayings of Jesus include three seed parables perhaps drawn from a collection of parables, a saying based on Isaiah 6:9–10, an allegory, and wisdom sayings.

10. This outline is a modification of one by Donahue, *Gospel in Parable,* 31.

I make a change to include v. 13 along with vv. 10–12 instead of with vv. 14–20 as he does. My reasons for doing so will follow.

11. See John Bowker, "Mystery and Parable: Mark iv. 1–20," *Journal of Theological Studies* 25 (1974): 305; and Joel Marcus, *The Mystery of the Kingdom of God,* SBL Dissertation Series 90 (Atlanta: Scholars Press, 1986), 46, for discussion of the Hebrew background of the word. See Vincent Taylor, *The Gospel according to St. Mark,* 2d ed., Thornapple Commentaries (1966; reprint, Grand Rapids: Baker Book House, 1981), 255, for its use in the New Testament.

12. Elisabeth Schüssler Fiorenza, *Jesus: Miriam's Child, Sophia's Prophet* (New York: Continuum, 1994), 92.

13. Ambrozic, *Hidden Kingdom,* 99; Cranfield, "Part 2," 53.

14. Schüssler Fiorenza, *Miriam's Child,* 92.

15. These phrases represent the respective interpretations of "those who are outside" by the following scholars: Ambrozic, *Hidden Kingdom,* 91; Donahue, *Gospel in Parable,* 44; Mary Ann Tolbert, *Sowing the Gospel: Mark's World in Literary-Historical Perspective* (Philadelphia: Fortress Press, 1989), 160; Morna Hooker, *The Message of Mark* (London: Epworth Press, 1983), 27.

16. Ambrozic, *Hidden Kingdom,* 80. Many people are uncomfortable with the idea that Jesus would speak in a way *so that* some would not repent. Some scholars have tried to find ways to soften the force of the Greek clause so that it does not mean "for the purpose of" preventing repentance. The most natural reading of the text, however, is as a purpose clause. See Taylor, *St. Mark,* 257; Craig A. Evans, "The Function of Isaiah 6:9–10 in Mark and John," *Novum Testamentum* 24 (1982): 132–33.

17. So Tolbert, *Sowing the Gospel,* 160–61: "The parables . . . do not force people outside or pull people inside; they simply reveal the type of ground already present"; and Marshall, *Faith as a Theme,* 65: "For someone who already perceives the hidden reality of God's rule in the events surrounding Jesus . . . the parables should further clarify that rule. But for those who do not discern God's presence in Jesus, the parables only obscure matters further."

18. Jean Leclerq, "Preface," in *Julian of Norwich: Showings,* ed. Edmund Colledge and James Walsh, The Classics of Western Spirituality (New York: Paulist Press, 1978), 5. In addition, Tolbert claimed, "Hearing the word is the crucial moment of revelation, and then how one responds to that hearing determines the result." *Sowing the Gospel,* 163.

19. These translations are drawn from A. E. J. Rawlinson, *St. Mark,* Westminster Commentaries (London: Methuen & Co., 1925), 53; Eduard Lohse, *Mark's Witness to Jesus Christ* (New York: Association Press, 1955), 74.

20. Taylor, *St. Mark,* 260.

21. "Heart" is actually not used in v. 17. Instead, Mark says these people have no root in themselves. But since "heart" in semitic thought refers to the personal center of a person where thoughts and decisions are

made, it seems to be what Mark intends by "in themselves." See Jan Lambrecht, "Jesus and the Law: An Investigation of Mk 7, 1–23," *Ephemerides theologicae lovanienses* 53 (1977): 47. As we will see, "heart" is a significant idea in Mark's thought. Indeed, we have already used it to speak of "outsiders" as those whose hearts are not open to God.

22. Ched Myers, *Binding the Strong Man: A Political Reading of Mark's Story of Jesus* (Maryknoll, N.Y.: Orbis Books, 1988), 175.

23. C.E.B. Cranfield, "St. Mark 4.1–34," part 1, *Scottish Journal of Theology* 4 (1951): 412; Birger Gerhardsson, "The Parable of the Sower and Its Interpretation," *New Testament Studies* 14 (1968): 182.

24. Myers, *Binding the Strong Man,* 177.

25. An aorist participle (*sparentes*) followed by the present tenses of hear (*akouousin*) and accept (*paradechontai*) emphasize the continual faithful and fruitful response. Anderson, *Mark,* 134.

26. A number of scholars view this parable similarly, including Robert A. Guelich, *Mark 1–8:26,* Word Biblical Commentary, vol. 34A (Dallas: Word Books, 1989), 231; J. R. Kirkland, "The Earliest Understanding of Jesus' Use of Parables: Mark IV 10–12 in Context," *Novum Testamentum* 19 (1977): 12–13; and Tolbert, *Sowing the Gospel,* 161.

27. Taylor, *St. Mark,* 365.

28. Peter Rhea Jones, "The Seed Parables of Mark," *Review and Expositor* 75 (1978): 523.

29. Marcus, *Mystery,* 216–17, noted that throughout Mark healthy plants symbolize the life-giving power of God's new age as in 4:8, 20 and 13:28–29. These are juxtaposed with unfruitful plants whose deadness evokes the sterility of the old age as in 4:4–7, 15–19, and 11:12–14, 20.

30. Donahue, *Gospel in Parable,* 38.

31. These observations regarding Mark's placement of the story are drawn from D. E. Nineham, *The Gospel of St. Mark,* Pelican Gospel Commentaries (London: Adam & Charles Black, 1963), 188; and Hooker, *Message,* 81.

32. For discussion of the composite nature of the passage, see Anderson, *Mark,* 180; B. Harvie Branscomb, *The Gospel of Mark,* Moffat New Testament Commentary (London: Hodder & Stoughton, 1937), 122; Charles Carlston, "The Things That Defile (Mark VII. 14) and the Law in Matthew and Mark," *New Testament Studies* 15 (1969): 91.

33. Lambrecht, "Jesus and the Law," 101.

34. Anderson, *Mark,* 183, noted that the reference to Jerusalem, the city of Jesus' death, heightens the sense of conflict in the story. See also Elizabeth Struthers Malbon, *Narrative Space and Mythic Meaning in Mark* (San Francisco: Harper & Row, 1986), 40–46, for discussion of the opposition between Galilee and Jerusalem in Mark.

35. Robert Banks, *Jesus and the Law in the Synoptic Tradition* (Cambridge: Cambridge University Press, 1975), 132.

36. Lambrecht, "Jesus and the Law," 55.

37. See Jacob Neusner, "Varieties of Judaism in the Formative Age," in *Jewish Spirituality: From the Bible to the Middle Ages,* ed. Arthur Green

(New York: Crossroad, 1987), 174; Sandra M. Schneiders, "Scripture and Spirituality," in *Christian Spirituality: Origins to the Twelfth Century,* ed. Bernard McGinn, John Meyendorff, Jean Leclerq (New York: Crossroad, 1985), 2–5. Both books are part of World Spirituality: An Encyclopedic History of the Religious Quest, vols. 13 and 16, respectively.

38. B. Harvie Branscomb, *Jesus and the Law of Moses* (New York: Richard R. Smith, 1930), 119.

39. Ibid., 96.

40. Madeleine Boucher, *The Mysterious Parable: A Literary Study,* Catholic Biblical Quarterly Monograph Series 6 (Washington, D.C.: Catholic Biblical Association of America, 1977), 65.

41. Lambrecht, "Jesus and the Law," 64.

42. Bruce J. Malina, *The New Testament World: Insights from Cultural Anthropology* (Atlanta: John Knox Press, 1981), 131–134, gives detailed descriptions of genealogical purity lines in ancient Israel.

43. Jerome H. Neyrey, "A Symbolic Approach to Mark 7," *Forum* 4 (1989): 77.

44. Bruce J. Malina and Richard Rohrbaugh, *Social Science Commentary on the Synoptic Gospels* (Minneapolis: Augsburg Fortress, 1992), 221, note that farmers and fishermen are among those whose occupations would not allow them to keep these purity traditions.

45. Carlston, "Things That Defile," 95; Branscomb, *Jesus,* 118.

46. Jon Michael Stubblefield, "Mark 7:1–23 in Light of the First Century Understanding of Clean-Unclean" (Ph.D. diss., The Southern Baptist Theological Seminary, 1975), demonstrated that ritual purity was an important concept in Judaism and the religions of the Greco-Roman world, 51–76, and that food regulations were widely practiced by both Jews and Gentiles in the first century C.E., 138–43.

47. C. S. Mann, *Mark,* Anchor Bible, vol. 27 (Garden City, N.Y.: Doubleday & Co., 1986), 315–16. The categories of "acts" and "vices" are Mann's as are the translations of them presented here.

48. Schweizer, *Mark,* 147–48; Stephen Westerholm, *Jesus and Scribal Authority,* Coniectanea Biblica, New Testament Series 10 (Lund: Lund University, 1978), 80.

Notes to Chapter 3

1. See the following, among many possibilities, for this view of miracles in Mark: Aloysius M. Ambrozic, "New Teaching with Power," in *Word and Spirit: Essays in Honor of David Michael Stanley, S.J., on His 60th Birthday,* ed. Joseph Plevnik (Ontario: Regis College Press, 1975), 139; Christopher D. Marshall, *Faith as a Theme in Mark's Narrative* (Cambridge: Cambridge University Press, 1989), 61–71; D. E. Nineham, *The Gospel of St. Mark,* Pelican Gospel Commentaries (London: Adam & Charles Black, 1963), 211; and Augustine Stock, *Call to Dis-*

cipleship: A Literary Study of Mark's Gospel, Good News Studies 1 (Wilmington: Michael Glazier, 1982), 77.

2. See Morna D. Hooker, *The Message of Mark* (London: Epworth Press, 1983), 41; and C. S. Mann, *Mark,* Anchor Bible, vol. 27 (Garden City, N.Y.: Doubleday & Co., 1986), 141, for this perspective on miracles in Mark.

3. Herman Hendrickx, *The Miracle Stories* (San Francisco: Harper & Row, 1987), 12; H. van der Loos, *The Miracles of Jesus* (Leiden: E. J. Brill, 1965), 351.

4. Antoinette Clark Wire, "The Structure of the Gospel Miracle Stories and Their Tellers," *Semeia* 11 (1978): 109.

5. Joanna Dewey, "The Literary Structure of the Controversy Stories in Mark 2:1–3:6," in *The Interpretation of Mark,* ed. William Telford (1973; reprint, Philadelphia: Fortress Press, 1985), 100.

6. The English translations do not do justice to the Greek in 3:3. Examples: the NRSV has "come forward"; the RSV has "come here"; the NIV has "stand up in front." While these translations make good English sense, they do not capture the clear resurrection overtones in the Greek verb *egeiro.* The literal translation would be "rise into the middle."

7. J. Duncan M. Derrett, "Christ and the Power of Choice (Mark 3, 1–6), *Biblica* 65 (1984): 172.

8. Mann, *Mark,* 241.

9. See, among others, Joanna Dewey, *Markan Public Debate: Literary Technique, Concentric Structure, and Theology in Mark 2:1–3:6,* SBL Dissertation Series 48 (Chico, Calif.: Scholars Press, 1980), 46; and Darrell J. Doughty, "The Authority of the Son of Man (Mk 2:1–3:6)," *Zeitschrift für die neutestamentliche Wissenschaft und die Kunde der alteren Kirche* 74 (1983), 174, for discussion of Mark's editorial activity here.

10. Harald Riesenfeld, "The Sabbath and the Lord's Day in Judaism, the Preaching of Jesus and Early Christianity," trans. E. Margaret Rowley, in *The Gospel Tradition* (1959; reprint, Philadelphia: Fortress Press, 1970), 112. See also Bruce J. Malina and Richard Rohrbaugh, *Social Science Commentary on the Synoptic Gospels* (Minneapolis: Augsburg Fortress, 1992), 221, on the difficulty many peasants had keeping the kosher tradition.

11. Derrett, "Power of Choice," 186; Eduard Schweizer, *The Good News according to Mark,* trans. Donald H. Madvig (Atlanta: John Knox Press, 1970), 75.

12. Schweizer, *Mark,* 75; Hendrickx, *Miracle Stories,* 151.

13. Van der Loos, *Miracles,* 216; Riesenfeld, "The Sabbath," 113–14, 118.

14. Riesenfeld, "The Sabbath," 119–22.

15. Denise Lardner Carmody, *Seizing the Apple: A Feminist Spirituality of Personal Growth* (New York: Crossroad, 1984), 19.

16. Ibid.

17. I am indebted to M. Eugene Boring, *Revelation,* Interpretation, A Bible Commentary for Teaching and Preaching (Louisville, Ky.: John Knox Press, 1989), 96, for this understanding of repentance as reorientation of life according to the teachings of the gospel.

18. Wire, "Structure," 96, claimed that the religious leaders created restrictions in God's name to maintain their order and privilege.

19. Kathleen M. Fisher and Urban C. von Wahlde, "The Miracles of Mark 4:35–5:43: Their Meaning and Function in the Gospel Framework," *Biblical Theology Bulletin* 11 (1981): 13–14; see also Eduard Schweizer, "The Portrayal of the Life of Faith in the Gospel of Mark," *Interpretation* 32 (1978): 395.

20. Robert Wayne Stacy, "Fear in the Gospel of Mark" (Ph.D. diss., The Southern Baptist Theological Seminary, 1980), 123; John R. Donahue, "Jesus as Parable of God in the Gospel of Mark," *Interpretation* 32 (1978): 381.

21. Howard Clark Kee, "The Terminology of Mark's Exorcism Stories," *New Testament Studies* 14 (1968): 242–44, studied the background of the Greek verb *epitamao* and concluded that "rebuke" (used by the NRSV) is a wholly inadequate translation. He claimed that only a paraphrase such as "the commanding word by which the representative of the forces opposed to God is overcome" (which is similar to the phrase I have used) catches the force of term.

22. Fisher and von Wahlde, "Miracles of Mark 4:35–5:43," 14.

23. Hooker, *Message,* 43; Nineham, *St. Mark,* 146; Paul J. Achtemeier, "Person and Deed: Jesus and the Storm-tossed Sea," *Interpretation* 16 (1962): 171–73.

24. Bernard F. Batto, "The Sleeping God: An Ancient Near Eastern Motif of Divine Sovereignty," *Biblica* 68 (1987): 173; Fisher and von Wahlde, "Miracles of Mark 4:35–5:43," 15.

25. A number of scholars have commented on the sense of the divine presence in this story: Achtemeier, "Person and Deed," 174; Batto, "The Sleeping God," 173; Hugh Anderson, *The Gospel of Mark,* New Century Bible Commentary (Grand Rapids: Wm. B. Eerdmans Publishing Co., 1976), 145; Van der Loos, *Miracles,* 655. Indeed, David E. Garland, "'I am the Lord Your Healer': Mark 1:21–2:12," *Review and Expositor* 85 (1988): 335–39, argued that in the miracles of 1:21–2:12 Mark has also pictured Jesus doing what God alone can do. It appears, therefore, that Mark is concerned to heighten the sense of the divine presence of Jesus throughout his story. Nowhere, however, is this heightening more prominent than in the stilling of the storm and the stupendous miracles that follow.

26. Batto, "The Sleeping God," 164, 175.

27. Anderson, *Mark,* 145; Schweizer, *Mark,* 109.

28. See Fisher and von Wahlde, "Miracles of Mark 4:35–5:43," p. 14; Sharyn Dowd, *Prayer, Power, and the Problem of Suffering,* SBL Dissertation Series 105 (Atlanta: Scholars Press, 1988) 107; James M. Robinson, *The Problem of History in Mark and Other Marcan Studies* (Philadelphia: Fortress Press, 1982), 121.

29. This understanding of numinous awe is taken from Rudolf Otto's classic *The Idea of the Holy,* 2d ed., trans. John W. Harvey (London: Oxford University, 1950). Numinous awe rises in the face of the holy or

mysterium tremendum or wholly other (p. 26), which is awful and dreadful but also uniquely fascinating and attracting (p. 31).

30. Schweizer, *Mark,* 110.

31. John R. Donahue, "The Revelation of God in the Gospel of Mark," in *Modern Scholarship: Its Impact on Theology and Proclamation,* ed. Francis A. Eigo (Villanova, Pa.: Villanova University Press, 1984), 160.

32. Otto, *Idea of the Holy,* 31.

33. For a detailed look at this woman's story, see my article "Old Stories Through New Eyes: Insights Gained from a Feminist Reading of Mark 5:25–34," *Memphis Theological Seminary Journal* 30 (1992): 2–14.

34. Edward D. O'Connor, *Faith in the Synoptic Gospels: A Problem in the Correlation of Scripture and Theology* (South Bend, Ind.: University of Notre Dame Press, 1961), 50.

35. Several scholars have noted these oddities. Gail R. O'Day, "Surprised by Faith: Jesus and the Canaanite Woman," *Listening: Journal of Religion and Culture* 24 (1989): 293, discusses ways the woman is the protagonist in Matthew's version of the story. Her observations are true of Mark's story also. Mary Ann Tolbert, "Mark," in *The Women's Bible Commentary,* ed. Carol A. Newsom and Sharon Ringe (Louisville, Ky.: Westminster/John Knox Press, 1992), 269; Ched Myers, *Binding the Strong Man: A Political Reading of Mark's Story of Jesus* (Maryknoll, N.Y.: Orbis Books, 1988), 204; Sharon H. Ringe, "A Gentile Woman's Story," in *Feminist Interpretation of the Bible,* ed. Letty M. Russell (Philadelphia: Westminster Press, 1985), 71; and Elisabeth Schüssler Fiorenza, "Commitment and Critical Inquiry: Harvard Divinity School 1988 Convocation," in *The Discipleship of Equals: A Critical Feminist Ekklesia-logy of Liberation* (New York: Crossroad, 1993), 289, all point out how the woman is the only person to best Jesus in an argument in Mark. Morna D. Hooker, *The Gospel according to St. Mark,* Black's New Testament Commentary (Peabody, Mass.: Hendrickson Publishers, 1991), 182, claims that the story presents Jesus as "churlish" and "erratic in the way in which he . . . changed his mind."

36. O'Day, "Surprised by Faith," 291.

37. Hisako Kinukawa, *Women and Jesus in Mark: A Japanese Feminist Perspective* (Maryknoll, N.Y.: Orbis Books, 1994), 53.

38. Kathleen E. Corley, *Private Women, Public Meals: Social Conflict in the Synoptic Tradition* (Peabody, Mass.: Hendrickson Publishers, 1993), 98; Robert A. Guelich, *Mark 1–8:26,* Word Biblical Commentary, vol. 34a (Dallas: Word Books, 1989), 385.

39. Kinukawa, *Women and Jesus,* 59; Ringe, "Gentile Woman's Story," 70.

40. Kinukawa, *Women and Jesus,* 55; Ringe, "Gentile Woman's Story," 70.

41. Kinukawa, *Women and Jesus,* 54; Myers, *Binding the Strong Man,* 203.

42. Ringe, "Gentile Woman's Story," 70.

43. Myers, *Binding the Strong Man,* 203.

44. Corley, *Private Women,* 99; O'Day, "Surprised by Faith," 297; Kinukawa, *Women and Jesus,* 55.

45. Ringe, "Gentile Woman's Story," 70–71.

46. Francis Dufton, "The Syrophoenician Woman and Her Dogs," *Expository Times* 100 (1989): 417, notes the cultural differences between Jews' and Gentiles' attitudes toward dogs. While they might be pets for Gentiles, for Jews they were dirty, savage dogs roaming the streets in packs scavenging for food.
47. O'Day, "Surprised by Faith," 297; Kinukawa, *Women and Jesus,* 58.
48. Kinukawa, *Women and Jesus,* 59.
49. Ringe, "Gentile Woman's Story," 71; Kinukawa, *Women and Jesus,* 60; O'Day, "Surprised by Faith," 299.
50. Mitzi Minor, "The Women of the Gospel of Mark and Contemporary Women's Spirituality," *Spirituality Today* 43 (1991): 138; Bruce J. Malina, *The New Testament World: Insights from Cultural Anthropology* (Atlanta: John Knox Press, 1981), 30–32.
51. Kinukawa, *Women and Jesus,* 60–61.
52. Ringe, "Gentile Woman's Story," 71.
53. O'Day, "Surprised by Faith," 299.

Notes to Chapter 4

1. Ernest Best, *Following Jesus: Discipleship in the Gospel of Mark* (Sheffield: JSOT Press, 1981), 15–16. This type of spiritual understanding of "the way" is not unique to Mark's Gospel. The metaphor of "journey" or "pilgrimage" or "way" has often been used for the life of faith from Abraham going out by faith, the wilderness wanderings, and the return from Babylonian captivity in the Hebrew Bible through Bonaventure's *Itinerarium mentis in Deum* to Bunyan's *Pilgrim's Progress.* It is, it seems, entirely scriptural: the people of God seeking a country, Jesus in John's Gospel going ahead to prepare a place for his disciples in God's house, Mark's Jesus going ahead to Jerusalem. The Acts of the Apostles notes that Christians were called followers of "the Way" (e.g., 9:2). Christian mystics have often taught a mystical way to God. See Gordon S. Wakefield, "Pilgrimmage," in *The Westminster Dictionary of Christian Spirituality,* ed. Gordon S. Wakefield (Philadelphia: Westminster Press, 1983), 302. For these reasons, and because of the sigificance of the term "the way" for Mark, I have named authentic spirituality according to Mark "The Way of the Lord."
2. See Best, *Following Jesus,* 24–25; Eduard Schweizer, *The Good News According to Mark,* trans. Donald H. Madvig (Atlanta: John Knox Press, 1970), 191, 218; Paul J. Achtemeier, "Mark 9:30–37," *Interpretation* 30 (1976): 178.
3. I have long wrestled with "inclusivizing" Son of man. As a feminist who appreciates the power of language, I insist that it must be done. But as someone also aware of the wide usage of the title in Christian liturgy, I know it must be done well, and I have not been sold on any of the options scholars have used to this point. My study of this Gospel leads me to believe that "New Human Being" is closest to what Mark

meant by Son of man, but would nonspecialists read New Human Being and understand that what has been replaced is Son of man? I fear not. Hence I have chosen to "slash it": Son of man/New Human Being. This form is cumbersome, but I hope it will be clearer for readers.

4. D. E. Nineham, *The Gospel of St. Mark,* Pelican Gospel Commentaries (London: Adam & Charles Black, 1963), 225.

5. Elisabeth Schüssler Fiorenza, *Jesus: Miriam's Child, Sophia's Prophet* (New York: Continuum, 1994), 101, points out that our language about God and Jesus' death can indeed paint such a picture of God. Worse, some victims of abuse and violence at the hand of Christians (persons during the Crusades, slaves, abused wives and children, etc.) may feel that they had indeed experienced God as cruel. I believe Mark would say, and I would agree, that those Christians who choose violence do so at their own accord, that God is absolutely opposed to oppression and violence against anyone.

6. Ched Myers, *Binding the Strong Man: A Political Reading of Mark's Story of Jesus* (Maryknoll, N.Y.: Orbis Books, 1988), 244.

7. Mary Ann Tolbert, *Sowing the Gospel: Mark's World in Literary-Historical Perspective* (Philadelphia: Fortress Press, 1989), 236–37.

8. E.g., Myers, *Binding the Strong Man,* 308; William R. Herzog II, *Parables as Subversive Speech: Jesus as Pedagogue of the Oppressed* (Louisville, Ky.: Westminster/John Knox Press, 1994), 101–4.

9. Myers, *Binding the Strong Man,* 308.

10. Tolbert, *Sowing the Gospel,* 238.

11. Herman C. Waetjen, *A Reordering of Power: A Socio-Political Reading of Mark's Gospel* (Minneapolis: Fortress Press, 1989), 145–46, speaks of Jesus' death at the hands of the elites similarly to the way I have here.

12. Aaron Milavec, "The Identity of 'the Son' and 'the Others': Mark's Parable of the Wicked Husbandmen Reconsidered," *Biblical Theology Bulletin* 20 (1990): 34.

13. Barnabas Lindars, "Salvation Proclaimed. Mark X.45: A Ransom for Many," *Expository Times* 93 (1982): 295; Vincent Taylor, *Jesus and His Sacrifice: A Study of the Passion-Sayings in the Gospels* (London: Macmillan & Co., 1937), 103; Adela Yarbro Collins, *The Beginning of the Gospel: Probings of Mark in Context* (Minneapolis: Fortress Press, 1992), 69.

14. E.g., A. E. J. Rawlinson, *St. Mark,* Westminster Commentaries (London: Methuen & Co., 1925), 147; James A. Brooks, *Mark,* New American Commentary (Nashville: Broadman Press, 1991), 171.

15. Elisabeth Schüssler Fiorenza, *In Memory of Her: A Feminist Theological Reconstruction of Christian Origins* (New York: Crossroad, 1983), 128; Bruce J. Malina and Richard Rohrbaugh, *Social Science Commentary on the Synoptic Gospels* (Minneapolis: Augsburg Fortress, 1992), 188–189, point out that the introspective, guilt-oriented outlook toward sin of industrialized societies did not exist in the first-century Mediterranean world, that "conscience" was not an interior voice of accusation but an external one that came from what others said.

16. I am indebted to my friend Dr. Chris Church for this insight into Mark's use of an exodus rather than a sacrifice of atonement motif.

17. James L. Mays, "Mark 8:27–9:1," *Interpretation* 30 (1976): 176.

18. Howard Clark Kee, *Community of the New Age: Studies in Mark's Gospel* (1977; reprint, Macon, Ga.: Mercer University Press, 1983), 116.

19. Mays, "Mark 8:27–9:1," 176.

20. John R. Donahue, *The Theology and Setting of Discipleship in the Gospel of Mark* (Milwaukee: Marquette University Press, 1983), 47–48.

21. Robert C. Tannehill, "Reading It Whole: The Function of Mark 8:34–35 in Mark's Story," *Quarterly Review* 2 (1982): 68.

22. Nineham, *Mark,* 226.

23. Myers, *Binding the Strong Man,* 245; Martin Hengel, *Crucifixion* (Philadelphia: Fortress Press, 1978), 86.

24. John D. Zizioulas, "The Early Christian Community," in *Christian Spirituality: Origins to the Twelfth Century,* ed. Bernard McGinn, John Meyendorff, Jean Leclerq, World Spirituality: An Encyclopedic History of the Religious Quest, vol. 16 (New York: Crossroad, 1985), 24.

25. Myers, *Binding the Strong Man,* 247.

26. Achtemeier, "Mark 9:30–37," 182. Malina and Rohrbaugh, *Social Science Commentary,* 238, note that children had little status in the families of that time. "A minor child was on a par with a slave, and only after reaching maturity was he/she a free person who could inherit the family estate. The term 'child/children' could also be used as a serious insult (see Matt. 11:16–17)."

27. Achtemeier, "Mark 9:30–37," 182.

28. Dan O. Via, *The Ethics of Mark's Gospel—In the Middle of Time* (Philadelphia: Fortress Press, 1985), 158.

29. Elisabeth Schüssler Fiorenza, "Gather in My Name: Toward a Christian Feminist Spirituality," in *Discipleship of Equals: A Critical Feminist Ekklesia-logy of Liberation* (New York: Crossroad, 1993), 198–99.

30. Best, *Following Jesus,* 126; Joanna Dewey, *Disciples of the Way: Mark on Discipleship* (Women's Division, Board of Global Ministries, The United Methodist Church, 1976), 92.

31. Elisabeth Schüssler Fiorenza, "Patriarchal Structures and the Discipleship of Equals" and "Feminist Ministry in the Discipleship of Equals," in *Discipleship of Equals,* 220–21, 305, respectively. The phrase "discipleship of equals" is closely tied to Schüssler Fiorenza's work.

32. David Rhoads and Donald Michie, *Mark as Story* (Philadelphia: Fortress Press, 1982), 109–11.

33. Hendrikus Boers, "Reflections on the Gospel of Mark: A Structural Investigation," in *SBL 1987 Seminar Papers,* ed. Kent Harold Richards (Atlanta: Scholars Press, 1987), 265.

34. There is a growing body of literature on this view women often have of themselves. See my articles, "The Women of the Gospel of Mark and Contemporary Women's Spirituality," *Spirituality Today* 43 (1991), and "Old Stories Through New Eyes: Insights Gained from a Feminist Reading of Mark 5:25–34," *Memphis Theological Seminary Journal* 30 (1992), and the bibliographies of each.

35. Willi Marxsen, *Mark the Evangelist: Studies in the Redaction History of the Gospel,* trans. James Boyce, Donald Juel, William Poehlmann, Roy A. Harrisville (Nashville: Abingdon Press, 1969), 166–67; Hugh Anderson, *The Gospel of Mark,* New Century Bible Commentary (Grand Rapids: Wm. B. Eerdmans Publishing Co., 1976), 288. While scholars generally agree that Mark 13 is the evangelist's own construction, there are no agreements on the sources he used to compose it. Those interested in the question of sources may consult G. R. Beasley-Murray, *Jesus and the Future* (London: Macmillan & Co., 1954), 1–79; Rudolf Pesch, *Naherwartungen: Tradition und Redaktion in Mk 13* (Dusseldorf: Patmos Verlag, 1968); Jan Lambrecht, *Die Redaktion der Markus-Apokalypse: Literarische Analyse und Strukturuntersuchung,* Analecta biblica 28 (Rome: Papstliches Bibelinstitut, 1967).

36. Elisabeth Schüssler Fiorenza, *The Book of Revelation: Justice and Judgement* (Philadelphia: Fortress Press, 1985), 54, 186–87; Eugene H. Petersen, *Reversed Thunder: The Revelation of John and the Praying Imagination* (San Francisco: Harper & Row, 1988), 14–15.

37. Charles B. Cousar, "Eschatology and Mark's *Theologia Crucis:* A Critical Analysis of Mark 13," *Interpretation* 24 (1970): 328–29; Marxsen, *Mark the Evangelist,* 173; Morna D. Hooker, "Trial and Tribulation in Mark XIII," *Bulletin of the John Rylands University Library* 65 (1982): 88.

38. Morna D. Hooker, *The Message of Mark* (London: Epworth Press, 1983), 115.

39. R.H. Lightfoot, *The Gospel Message of St. Mark* (Oxford: Clarendon Press, 1950), 49–50.

40. Waetjen, *Reordering of Power,* 197. As Mark wrote (scholarly consensus holds to a date between 65 and 70 C.E.), the Temple may have been on the verge of destruction or already have been destroyed as a result of the Jewish revolt against Rome in 66 C.E., an event that could have spawned intense apocalyptic speculation. See Myers, *Binding the Strong Man,* 64–69, for a description of the key role played by the Temple in the revolt that led to its destruction.

41. George R. Beasley-Murray, *A Commentary on Mark 13* (London: Macmillan & Co., 1957), 49.

42. Elisabeth Schüssler Fiorenza, *Revelation: Vision of a Just World,* Proclamation Commentaries (Minneapolis: Fortress Press, 1991), 51.

43. John R. Donahue, *The Gospel in Parable: Metaphor, Narrative, and Theology in the Synoptic Gospels* (Philadelphia: Fortress Press, 1988), 58. The statement that "this generation will not pass away until these things happen" (13:30) is in some tension with the statement that no one knows the exact hour except God (v. 32). Cousar, "Eschatology," 325, made the plausible suggestion that the tension was intentional so as to relativize and broaden the phrase "this generation" and make the discourse applicable to Mark's own generation and perhaps others following. Thus, according to Beasley-Murray, *Commentary,* 105, the evangelist declares two certain features of the parousia: it comes, but no human being knows when it comes.

44. Donald H. Juel, *A Master of Surprise: Mark Interpreted* (Minneapolis: Augsburg Fortress, 1994), 86.
45. Anderson, *Mark,* 301.
46. Zizioulas, "Early Christian Community," 23–24.
47. David S. Lull, "Interpreting Mark's Story of Jesus's Death: Toward a Theology of Suffering," *SBL 1985 Seminar Papers,* ed. Kent Harold Richards (Atlanta: Scholars Press, 1985), 3–4. See also Luke Timothy Johnson, *The Writings of the New Testament: An Interpretation* (Philadelphia: Fortress Press, 1986), 49.
48. Lars Hartman, *Prophecy Interpreted,* trans. Neil Tomkinson and Jean Gray (Uppsala, Sweden: Almqvist & Wiksells, 1966), 152, noted that scholars are unsure of what exactly is meant by the abomination of desolation. His cautious statement that the symbol refers to some form of blasphemy seems to cover all the possibilities.
49. Hooker, "Trial," 91.
50. Eugene Petersen, *Reversed Thunder,* 20–21.

Notes to Chapter 5

1. D. E. Nineham, *The Gospel of St. Mark,* Pelican Gospel Commentaries (London: Adam & Charles Black, 1963), 242; Ernest Best, "The Miracles in Mark," *Review and Expositor* 75 (1978): 544.
2. The conclusion of the story in 9:28–29, like the introduction in v. 14, is generally considered to be Markan composition. Those interested in such matters may consult Ernest Best, *Following Jesus: Discipleship in the Gospel of Mark* (Sheffield: JSOT Press, 1981), 66; Paul J. Achtemeier, "Miracles and the Historical Jesus: A Study of Mark 9:14–29," *Catholic Biblical Quarterly* 37 (1975): 475; Sharyn Dowd, *Prayer, Power and the Problem of Suffering: Mark 11:22–25 in the Context of Markan Theology,* SBL Dissertation Series 105 (Atlanta: Scholars Press, 1988), 118.
3. Achtemeier, "Miracles," 476.
4. F. G. Lang, "Sola Gratia im Markusevangelium: Die Soteriologie des Markus nach 9, 14–29 und 10, 17–31," in *Rechtfertigung: Festschrift für Ernst Kasemann,* ed. J. Friedrich, W. Pöhlmann, Peter Stuhlmacher (Tübingen: J. C. B. Mohr [Paul Siebeck], 1976), 322.
5. See, e.g., Louis Bouyer, *The Spirituality of the New Testament and the Fathers,* A History of Christian Spirituality, vol. 1, trans. Mary Ryan (1960; reprint, Minneapolis: Winston Press, 1963), 109.
6. Herman C. Waetjen, *A Reordering of Power: A Socio-Political Reading of Mark's Gospel* (Minneapolis: Fortress Press, 1989), 115–17; Ched Myers, *Binding the Strong Man: A Political Reading of Mark's Story of Jesus* (Maryknoll, N.Y.: Orbis Books, 1988), 191. Myers gives notes about other military terms in the story.
7. Myers, *Binding the Strong Man,* 142, calls the last two approaches crude historicism and typically modernist approaches "preoccupied with con-

cocting rational explanations for actions that appear to transgress natural laws."

8. I use the phrase "power of the story" to indicate the impact it has on readers. Others might prefer "function of the story," or even "meaning of the story."

9. The rapid growth of the New Age movement, a number of best-selling books on angels as I write these words (spring 1995), the wide popularity of works by M. Scott Peck and Thomas More among others, and a growing interest among Christians about prayer and spirituality, which contributed to my desire to write this book are among the things that lead many people to believe there is a burgeoning contemporary interest in spirituality. See, e.g., Ewert Cousins, "Preface to the Series," *World Spirituality: An Encyclopedic History of the Religious Quest*, vols. 1–25 (New York: Crossroad).

10. This description of evil as a "dehumanizing power not under our control" is taken from Elisabeth Schüssler Fiorenza, *In Memory of Her: A Feminist Theological Reconstruction of Christian Origins* (New York: Crossroad, 1983), 123.

11. C. E. B. Cranfield, *The Gospel According to Saint Mark*, Cambridge Greek Testament Commentary (Cambridge: University Press, 1966), 301, suggested translations like "becomes stiff" or "becomes exhausted," but then admitted the difficulty in knowing how to translate this word in this context.

12. "Raised him up" is my translation of the Greek verb *egeiro*. "He arose" is my translation of *anistemi*. These verbs are the ones commonly used of Jesus' resurrection. Thus they continue the play between life and death in the passage. The NRSV translation, "Jesus took him by the hand and lifted him up, and he was able to stand" while making perfect sense of what was happening in the story, misses Mark's use of resurrection language entirely.

13. Nineham, *St. Mark,* 243.

14. Dowd, *Prayer,* 117; C. S. Mann, *Mark,* Anchor Bible, vol. 27 (Garden City, N.Y.: Doubleday & Co., 1986), 371; Vincent Taylor, *The Gospel according to St. Mark,* 2d ed., Thornapple Commentaries (1966; reprint, Grand Rapids: Baker Book House, 1981), 401.

15. My view here is similar to that of Myers, *Binding the Strong Man,* 255.

16. Cranfield, *Saint Mark,* 305, suggested the disciples may have thought God's power was now in their control, at their disposal.

17. Dowd, *Prayer,* 71–72. *Adynaton* is a transliteration of the Greek word for "not possible."

18. Edward D. O'Connor, *Faith in the Synoptic Gospels: A Problem in the Correlation of Scripture and Theology* (South Bend, Ind.: University of Notre Dame Press, 1961), 14; H. van der Loos, *The Miracles of Jesus* (Leiden: E. J. Brill, 1965), 400.

19. I would add here that I believe Mark would not include in "all things" any selfish prayers for such things as wealth, possessions, job advancement for the sake of advancement, and so on. These do not free others

and often clutter the lives of those who have them. I believe Mark
would concur with James 4:1–3.

20. Dowd, *Prayer,* examined the role of faith in the miracle stories, 107–14,
and concluded that sometimes in Mark faith leads to miracles, sometimes miracles lead to faith, and that the narrative preserves the freedom
of God to intervene even when unbelief is present. My understanding
of Jesus' response to the father's cry concurs with hers.

21. Donald Juel, *Messiah and Temple: The Trial of Jesus in the Gospel of Mark,*
SBL Dissertation Series 31 (Missoula, Mont.: Scholars Press, 1977),
133–34.

22. See William R. Telford, *The Barren Temple and the Withered Tree,* Journal for the Study of the New Testament, Supplement Series 1
(Sheffield: JSOT Press, 1980), 45, for indications that v. 11 is Mark's
handiwork.

23. C. K. Barrett, "The House of Prayer and the Den of Thieves," in *Jesus
and Paulus: Festschrift für Werner Georg Kummel,* ed. E. Earle Ellis and
Erich Grasser (Göttingen: Vandenhoeck & Ruprecht, 1975), 13–14;
Telford, *Barren Temple,* 46; Dowd, *Prayer,* 57; and Taylor, *St. Mark,*
465.

24. This outline is adapted from the work of Sharyn Dowd, *Prayer,* 38.

25. Ibid., 38–39.

26. The curious statement, "It was not the time for figs," has confounded
scholars for a long time. Some have tried to deal with it by claiming
that it is an accommodation made when the story was moved from its
original (historical) setting in the Feast of Tabernacles to the time of
Passover. Cf. T. W. Manson, "The Cleansing of the Temple," *Bulletin
of the John Rylands University Library,* 33 (1951): 271–82. Others have
argued that Jesus expected to find fruit because in the New Age the
trees will offer their fruit not as a matter of biological cycle but in response to the needs of the righteous, and Jesus considered the New Age
to have begun. Cf. Mann, *Mark,* 441; J. D. M. Derrett, "Fig Trees in
the New Testament," *The Heythrop Journal* 14 (1973): 254–58; Richard
B. Hiers, "Not the Season for Figs," *Journal of Biblical Literature,* 87
(1968): 395. I believe there is a better explanation that will be presented
later.

27. Dowd, *Prayer,* 119–20. That Greek form is optative mood.

28. See Telford, *Barren Temple,* 161–62; Derrett, "Fig Trees," 253; and
A. de Q. Robin, "The Cursing of the Fig Tree in Mark XI: A Hypothesis," *New Testament Studies* 8 (1962): 279, for discussion of trees,
figs, and fig trees as symbols in the Hebrew Scriptures and the New
Testament.

29. Myers, *Binding the Strong Man,* 300–301. For a more detailed look at
the redistribution economy of the Temple, see John H. Elliot, "Temple Versus Household in Luke-Acts: A Contrast in Social Institutions,"
in *The Social World of Luke-Acts: Models for Interpretation,* ed. Jerome H.
Neyrey (Peabody, Mass.: Hendrickson Publishers, 1991), 233–35.

30. Elliot, "Temple Versus Household," 235.

31. A growing number of scholars are reading the widow's story in this way. See Myers, *Binding the Strong Man*, 320–21; A. Wright, "The Widow's Mite: Praise or Lament? A Matter of Context," *Catholic Biblical Quarterly* 44 (1982): 262.

32. The class was Introduction to Church History taught by Dr. Penrose St. Amant at Southern Baptist Theological Seminary in Louisville, Kentucky (before the fundamentalist purge), in the spring of 1983. I was a student in that class.

33. Robin, "The Cursing," 279.

34. Joanna Dewey, *Markan Public Debate: Literary Technique, Concentric Structure, and Theology in Mark 2:1–3:3*, SBL Dissertation Series 48 (Chico, Calif.: Scholars Press, 1980), 57, claimed the phrase "it was no longer the time for figs" is a literary device indicating it is no longer the season for Israel. Though I would say the phrase indicates it is no longer the season for the Temple, I find her argument in favor of a literary device persuasive.

35. Barrett, "House of Prayer," 15; Dowd, *Prayer*, 45. Patrick D. Miller, *They Cried to the Lord: The Form and Theology of Biblical Prayer* (Minneapolis: Fortress Press, 1994), 48, 196–98, points out that while prayer was not limited to the Temple, the Temple was certainly a place for prayers to be heard.

36. This is a phrase from one of my professors, R. Alan Culpepper, "Mark 11:15–19," *Interpretation* 34 (1980): 177.

37. Taylor, *St. Mark*, 464; Mann, *Mark*, 449.

38. Mark's use of the Greek word *hieron* (temple) rather than *naos* (sanctuary) supports this view. See Juel, *Messiah and Temple*, 128.

39. Bruce J. Malina and Richard L. Rohrbaugh, *Social Science Commentary on the Synoptic Gospels* (Minneapolis: Augsburg Fortress Press, 1992), 59, claimed that some ancient prayers consisted of litanies, "often of great length, intended to tire the divinity so that she/he would grant the favor sought," while the formula for others called for the item sought to be described as exactly as possible lest the deity grant the wrong favor. Mark's Jesus does not teach these or any other ways to pray here so that the emphasis might fall on the one praying. Instead, as Miller, *They Cried to the Lord*, 310, noted, these teachings are "as much about the nature of God as they are about the possibility of prayer."

40. The verb translated doubt, *diakrino*, is concerned with judgment, discernment, decision. Christians appropriated the middle voice, which is usually translated "to doubt," to carry the sense of being inwardly divided or uncertain. See Dowd, *Prayer*, 104; Mann, *Mark*, 453; Taylor, *St. Mark*, 466. Malina and Rohrbaugh, *Social Science Commentary*, 252, suggested the verb for doubt means hesitancy in this context.

41. Dowd, *Prayer*, 104.

42. See, e.g., Edwin K. Broadhead, "Which Mountain Is 'This Mountain'? A Critical Note on Mark 11:22–25," *Paradigms* 2 (1986): 34–35; Myers, *Binding the Strong Man*, 305; Telford, *Barren Temple*, 118–19, who

notes that the Temple was known to the Jewish people as "this mountain."

43. Malina and Rohrbaugh, *Social Science Commentary,* 250.
44. John Paul Heil, *The Gospel of Mark as a Model for Action* (New York: Paulist Press, 1992), 230–31
45. Miller, *They Cried to the Lord,* 431; Mary Rose D'Angelo, "Theology in Mark and Q: *Abba* and 'Father' in Context," *Harvard Theological Review* 85 (1992): 158.

Notes to Conclusion

1. John R. Donahue, "A Neglected Factor in the Theology of Mark," *Journal of Biblical Literature* 101 (1982): 563–94.
2. Frederick Buechner, *Wishful Thinking: A Theological ABC* (New York: Harper & Row, 1973), 26.
3. Like most contemporary students of Mark's Gospel, I am persuaded that Mark's Gospel ended at 16:8, which means Mark related no resurrection appearances.
4. Bruce J. Malina, "'Let Him Deny Himself' (Mark 8:34 & Par): A Social and Psychological Model of Self-Denial," *Biblical Theology Bulletin* 24 (1994): 106–19, maintains that contemporary, individualistic understandings of the self appear to have been unknown in the ancient Mediterranean world. Instead, that world experienced the "collectivist self" which drew identity from one's group, especially one's family. Thus Malina claims, "As the synoptic tradition itself reveals, self-denial is family denial" (118). I have always wondered if Malina doesn't overstate his case, if it is possible for a person to have no sense of herself or himself as an individual. Nonetheless, he has shown the importance of remembering the significance of one's group to the people to whom Mark wrote. Thus I have named this category of responses "Focus on One's Own or *One's Group's* Interests."
5. There has been a wealth of study on the role of the disciples in Mark. Some scholars view them as total failures. Others see their narrative function as more ambiguous, a view I find more persuasive. See, e.g., Elizabeth Struthers Malbon, "Fallible Followers: Women and Men in the Gospel of Mark," *Semeia* 28 (1983): 29–48, and "Disciples/ Crowds/Whoever: Markan Characters and Readers," *Novum Testamentum* 28 (1986): 104–30 (I find Malbon's work to be particularly helpful); Robert C. Tannehill, "The Disciples in Mark: The Function of a Narrative Role," *Journal of Religion* 57 (1977): 386–405.
6. Several scholars have noted the likelihood that readers will identify most with the disciples in Mark's story. See, e.g., Tannehill, "The Disciples in Mark."
7. I freely, even gladly, acknowledge that the judgment of certain aspects of Mark's spirituality as "gems" is based on my own experiences of God, world, and self. These experiences have often been for me quite

significant, but they are also limited by the fact that I am a white, middle-class, North American woman who is an academic, an ordained Cumberland Presbyterian minister, and a feminist. These biases will, no doubt, be evident in what follows. I invite readers to name their own biases and see how these influence their interaction with Mark.

8. For full and excellent treatments of the issue of women's self-negation, see Valerie Saiving, "The Human Situation: A Feminist View," in *WomanSpirit Rising,* ed. Carol P. Christ and Judith Plaskow (San Francisco: Harper & Row, 1979), 25–42; and Susan Nelson Dunfee, "The Sin of Hiding: A Feminist Critique of Reinhold Niebuhr's Account of the Sin of Pride," *Soundings* 65 (1982): 316–27, among many others. For a discussion of how Jesus' treatment of women in Mark does not allow for their self-negation, see my article, "The Women of the Gospel of Mark and Contemporary Women's Spirituality," *Spirituality Today* 43 (1991): 134–41.

9. Elisabeth Schüssler Fiorenza, *In Memory of Her: A Feminist Theological Reconstruction of Christian Origins* (New York: Crossroad, 1983), chaps. 3, 7, and 8, discusses the gradual patriarchialization of the church that began near the end of the first century but met resistance into the fourth century.

10. Dana Stabenow, *Play with Fire* (New York: Berkley Publishing Group, 1995), 170. Note also the following from Karen Kijewski's recent popular mystery novel, *Alley Kat Blues* (New York: Doubleday, 1995), 69: "I thought religions were supposed to be about love." Her voice was tough and angry. I shrugged sympathetically. I didn't get the connection but I disagreed with her. To my mind organized religion was about love in roughly the same way that the Mafia was about family. Not. "But religions are really about power and money and making people do things, things that maybe aren't even the best choice for them."

11. Scholars generally believe Mark's Gospel was written to a community that faced persecution and suffering for its faith in Jesus, usually either in Galilee as a result of the 66 C.E. Jewish Revolt (see, e.g., Ched Myers, *Binding the Strong Man: A Political Reading of Mark's Story of Jesus* [Maryknoll, N.Y.: Orbis Books, 1988], 39–87) or in Rome during the reign of Nero (see, e.g., Donald Senior, " 'With Swords and Clubs . . . ' The Setting of Mark's Community and His Critique of Abusive Power," *Biblical Theology Bulletin* 17 [1987]: 10–20). We should probably not be surprised that Mark's rhetoric is more extreme given the probable situation his community faced.

12. My source for this information about King's appearance at Southern Baptist Theological Seminary in 1962 is a sermon preached in the SBTS chapel by Dr. Bill Leonard during the time I was a student there. As Dr. Leonard finished relating the financial cost of King's coming, he said to the chapel audience, "Let us declare here and now that that was money well spent!" We in the chapel rose from our seats with a roar and applauded wildly. It was one of the most powerful worship moments I have ever experienced.

13. Elisabeth Schüssler Fiorenza, *The Discipleship of Equals: A Critical Feminist Ekklesia-logy of Liberation* (New York: Crossroad, 1993), 275–76.
14. I have made use of Rebecca S. Chopp's description of Moltmann's theology in her *The Praxis of Suffering* (Maryknoll, N.Y.: Orbis Books, 1986), 101, 105.
15. These words of Johann Baptist Metz are cited in ibid., 68.
16. Dorothee Soëlle, *Thinking About God: An Introduction to Theology* (Philadelphia: Trinity Press International, 1990), 140.
17. Martin Luther King Jr., *The Words of Martin Luther King Jr.*, ed. Coretta Scott King (New York: Newmarket Press, 1987), 80–81.

Scripture Index

Hebrew Scriptures